T0193339

"*Empathipedia* is brilliantly written with both light-hearted humor and great soulful wisdom. Dave Markowitz has lovingly gifted the world a comprehensive manual on the ABCs of successfully navigating life as an empath or highly sensitive person."

—Dannion Brinkley,
NY Times bestselling author of
Saved by the Light

"In the extraordinary book *Empathipedia*, Dave Markowitz, a gifted healer who has clearly found his true calling, is offering his gift to the rest of us. Every time I open this book I am struck by the power of Dave's words, as if in connecting with his true voice he is talking directly to me and the place that I am at in the moment. Not coming from mere intellectual understanding, what Dave has written is a living expression of a deep experiential realization that touches and awakens a similar place of knowing in the reader. This book is a living transmission of Dave's wisdom that can greatly support anyone's healing journey, regardless of what path they are following. I can't recommend *Empathipedia* highly enough."

—Paul Levy,
author of *Dispelling Wetiko* and
The Quantum Revelation

"Dave Markowitz has done it again! In his latest book to support empaths, the reader is given expanded tools and wisdom for how to navigate this planet as a Highly Sensitive being in a way that brings more joy, connection and delight. This book will make you laugh and bring you comfort as you feel more understood--while also understanding yourself more fully. It gives you powerful tools you can immediately put into action as a skilled empath!"

—Heather Kristian Strang, best-selling author of *Live Like You're on Vacation: An Oracle, Ecstatic Union with The Divine*, and *A Life of Magic: An Oracle for Spirit-Led Living*

"*Empathipedia* takes readers well beyond the current knowledge base and introduces new ways of thinking about—and healing—old problems. Who hasn't been overwhelmed and disoriented at some point? With these tools, you can learn how to prevent empathic overload and heal yourself from its effects. It is an absolute must-read for Empaths and HSPs!"

—Anakha Coman, Corporate Trainer, Creator of Awake at Work mindfulness program and Co-Author of *The Proof*

Empathipedia

Healing for Empaths
and
Highly Sensitive Persons

Dave Markowitz

BALBOA.
PRESS
A DIVISION OF HAY HOUSE

Balboa Press books may be ordered through booksellers or by contacting:

Balboa Press
A Division of Hay House
1663 Liberty Drive
Bloomington, IN 47403
www.balboapress.com
1 (877) 407-4847

Because of the dynamic nature of the Internet, any web addresses or links contained in this book may have changed since publication and may no longer be valid. The views expressed in this work are solely those of the author and do not necessarily reflect the views of the publisher, and the publisher hereby disclaims any responsibility for them.

The author of this book does not dispense medical advice or prescribe the use of any technique as a form of treatment for physical, emotional, or medical problems without the advice of a physician, either directly or indirectly. The intent of the author is only to offer information of a general nature to help you in your quest for emotional and spiritual well-being. In the event you use any of the information in this book for yourself, which is your constitutional right, the author and the publisher assume no responsibility for your actions.

Book cover designed by Glenn Wright
Image licensed by Danielle Winter
Edited by Nicky Leach

Print information available on the last page.

ISBN: 978-1-9822-0105-0 (sc)
ISBN: 978-1-9822-0106-7 (e)

Balboa Press rev. date: 05/11/2018

Gratitude to Source, my family, friends, clients,
all Empaths and HSPs, and to Maria
who supports me in ways I never thought possible.

In loving memory, this book is dedicated to Alice Levin

Contents

Introduction

How to Get the Most from Empathipedia

Don't believe a word I've written.

Why would I begin a self-help book with "Don't believe a word I've written"? Because I'm only coming from my own experience and those of the thousands of people I've been blessed to work with. If what is written here doesn't resonate with you, that only means there is no resonance, nothing else, and I wish you well on your journey elsewhere. That said, I'd like to share a tiny bit of my own journey here, so you get a better idea of whose words you're reading.

My Story

My first glimpse of an empath was in the original *Star Trek* series. Captain Kirk, Mr. Spock, Dr. McCoy, and a woman from another planet were captives of an alien race called Vians who wanted to explore the concept of empathy. The woman, named Gem by Dr. McCoy, communicated nonverbally. She was an empath—someone who could feel the pain of others. But Gem took it one step farther: she could heal others by absorbing their pain and then transmute it! Perhaps curious about empathy because they appeared to have none, the Vians continually tested Gem's desire to experience the pain of others and heal them by progressively torturing the abducted members of the USS *Enterprise*.

While I'll assume many viewers thought, "How could those mean Vians do that to our heroes?" I thought, "Damn, wouldn't it be amazing to do what Gem does?" Who could have known that in a sense, I'd be doing what Gem does 40 years later?!?!

I didn't hear the word "empath" again for a few decades, even though I'd been living as one for so many years. The concept arose again after I became immersed in metaphysical communities in my late 30s, but I never inquired much beyond my sci-fi–infused understanding of the term.

After 45 years in and around New York City, Spirit suddenly said to me that it was time to go west. To that, like most New Yorkers would have, I replied, "Heck no!" But within three months, I was living in Portland, Oregon. Have you ever tried arguing with the Universe? Good luck with that!

Once here, I attended a MeetUp (through the online networking site meetup(dot)com, which matches groups of people with shared interests), and while I was there, a man approached me and told me I was an empath. Repeatedly. At that time, for whatever reason, I didn't want to own it. He sensed my hesitancy to believe him, so he said, "I'm the head of the (now defunct) Portland MeetUp for empaths. And I know an empath when I see one." But it wasn't until I had a more visceral experience with empathy that I would eventually buy into the label.

Being new to Portland and desiring camaraderie, I agreed to attend the birthday party of a friend of a friend. What I didn't know until I got there was that it was a party bus tour: seven bars in seven hours! And like many on the bus, at the end of the night I was drunk. Not atypical, right? But I hadn't drunk any alcohol. In that haze of post non-alcohol induced confusion came the clarity Spirit had been trying to tell me: I'm an empath. I'd absorbed the "drunk vibes" of all the people on the bus and in the various bars over the course of the evening.

With only a few exceptions, I hadn't been drunk since college. As the Chef from South Park says, "There's a time and place for everything, and it's called college." I quit for good in 2005, but this time I knew why I hated it so much. Bars are not good places for empaths!

From that point on, roughly 99 percent of the people who have come to me for intuitive guidance and healing facilitation have been empaths or Highly Sensitive Persons (HSPs).

Initially, I had no idea how to be a catalyst in healing others, but I'm a clear (enough) intuitive, and being open to assistance allowed vital information to flow through to me. I was then able to share that information with these HSPs and make useful recommendations about how they could heal. My main insight was that their symptoms were end results of consistently and empathically transmitted energies.

I saw that these new clients shared several common factors:

- Most, if not all, had already done a tremendous amount of healing work.
- They were for the most part, highly spiritual, and all had limited to no success permanently shifting what they were trying to heal.

- They all had an exceptionally high degree of responsibility for others.
- They were frustrated with their lack of personal progress and their limited ability to share their gifts with the world.

Working with these HSPs allowed me to intuit the Five Steps to Healing for the Highly Sensitive Person that later became the basis for my best-selling book, *Self-Care for the Self-Aware: A Guide for Highly Sensitive People, Empaths, Intuitives, and Healers.* I self-published the book in August 2013, which for 41 consecutive months remained in Amazon's Top 20 in its category.

People called me The Empath Guy. Seemingly overnight I'd become an expert on something that heretofore I hadn't even known existed outside of the world of *Star Trek.* I learned and then shared the differences between being an unskilled empath and a skilled empath, and guided each person from the former to the latter.

The Unskilled Empath vs. the Skilled Empath

The unskilled empath takes in whatever energies are coming their way and holds onto them. Over time, many empaths absorb others' energy to the point that they start to identify with what they're carrying. The unskilled empath can even be diagnosed by Western medicine as having a pain or illness, but one that was never theirs to carry! For the unskilled empath, empathy is a burden and can be a major factor in unhappiness and illness.

The skilled empath allows themself to experience the energy of the pain of others in order to express compassion and create deep connection. This is the *modus operandi* of many empaths, but the skilled empath knows that the incoming energy is not theirs to carry. Instead, they can have a momentary experience of the emotional state of whoever is in front of them without needing to fix it, and can therefore let that energy go through them. The skilled empath sees their abilities as a gift.

Once you have the tools, it's only a matter of practicing them until they become second nature. And even if you don't get to the level of mastery, an empath at any skill level can benefit greatly from the techniques in *Empathipedia*. Please know that you don't have to master anything to get results!

Think of the tools for being a skilled empath as being more like brushing your teeth than painting your home. You brush your teeth a few times a day, right? Do you ever say, "I wish I didn't have to brush my teeth after meals?" Of course not. Because you know that brushing your teeth works. It's logical. And so are the tools for excelling as an empath. As far-right-brained as much of this is, the tools are linear and can appeal to even the most ardent of logical and reasoning left-brainers.

How Does This Book Differ from *Self-Care for the Self-Aware*?
In the years since *Self-Care for the Self-Aware* was written, I've learned a lot. *Empathipedia* will succinctly reiterate some of the basics from *Self-Care* as a foundation to build upon. *Empathipedia* adds more detailed information to further help healing and thriving for empaths and Highly Sensitive Persons. For example, Keyhole Version 2.0 gives the reader more than a one-dimensional

understanding by invoking movement, visualization, visceral sensation, vocalization, vibration, and sound in addition to conceptual awareness. This experiential, multi-layered approach fosters a deeper embodiment, which has already helped thousands of empaths and HSPs. Application of the information herein can help you improve all areas of your life. *Empathipedia* also includes intentional misspellings, storytelling, an emphasis on teamwork, an A to Z list of the most common challenges that empaths and HSPs face, and hopefully, better jokes.

How Does this Book Differ from Other Books on Being an Empath?

I don't know—I've never read any of them. But my clients have, and they say that this work is dramatically different from what's already out there—that it is far more effective and works on the causal level. This work is more than a general description of what it means to be an empath; it's a detailed explanation of how to prevent, manage, and heal empathic transmissions of energy that have manifested in pain and illness in empaths and Highly Sensitive Persons.

Intentional Misspellings in *Empathipedia*

In addition to sharing the tools for preventing and healing empathic transmissions that can lead to pain and illness, I will be discussing the numerous challenges and opportunities that we as empaths and HSPs face. You'll be reading about the most common ailments my clients deal with, but because I'm not a medical doctor I will not be using the traditional diagnoses that may have brought you to this work. I am not legally allowed to diagnose, make a prognosis, or even claim any cure for what ails you, so I won't. But I do address the possible underlying energetic, emotional, and other non-physical and lesser-known causes of your symptoms. Please know that this book is not intended to replace your physical, psychological, medical, pharmaceutical, or surgical treatment in any way, shape, or form and that it is always best to listen to your doctor.

In addition to the literal or figurative meanings of words, all words have an energetic correlation. Once we give in to any label or diagnosis, we can attune to the collective unconscious's understanding of those labels. In some cases that may be okay, but at other times, connecting with the most commonly understood beliefs in the collective unconscious can lead to a sense of hopelessness in your quest for healing.

For example, if you were to agree that you have X diagnosis, you will then be connected to the larger understandings and results of that belief. If the commonly believed success rate in reversing X is very small, you will be plugged into that specific belief, potentially resulting in a decreased chance to grow and heal. Avoiding the more common label is *not* meant to minimize your symptoms, or even for a moment to say, "It's all in your head," but rather to open to more possibilities for transformation and healing. Many of the people I work with have been told "It's all in your head" and not always with compassion, but to me if someone is experiencing symptoms—whether those symptoms can be seen by modern technology or not—it is very real for them. And if it is real to them, it is real to me. Minimizing a client's experience is not conducive to helping them feel seen and heard and does not foster trust in our relationship. Who am I to determine what someone else is feeling?

To that end, I will allude to but not directly focus on diagnoses typically given to those who are suffering and looking for help. For example, I will use the chapter titled Anxiet-me to describe the very real mental reaction to stress, and the chapter titled Fibro-not-my-algia to describe the common condition of extremely tight muscles that are often the end result of consistent empathic transmissions.

Storytelling

As someone on a path of personal growth, you already know that challenges arise for a reason. Growth rarely comes easily. Sadly, or not, we often miss the subtler clues, and it isn't until our more painful experiences arise that we finally learn what we need to learn. My hope is that by sharing information, along with more personal stories, you can prevent what happened to me (or others I've worked with) from happening to you.

Storytelling can evoke a visceral response; it ignites more than the linear mind and is therefore more memorable than technical verbiage on a page. Hopefully, these stories will inspire you to work through your challenges rather than give in or give up. These random life snippets will show you that you're not alone. Knowing others have walked this path and have not only survived but actually thrived can be the difference between giving up all hope for healing and acknowledging and following our inherent impulse to evolve.

Teamwork

This may sound odd coming from a guy who wrote a book called *Self-Care for the Self-Aware* but over the past couple of decades, authors of self-help books—all well intentioned—have in many cases actually disempowered the reader.

Many empaths and HSPs (and many others, of course) have dealt with their fair share of codependency, and that birthed a part of the self-help model that promised to rectify codependency and the inherent problems associated within that framework. The ego, knowing codependency didn't work, figured, "Of course, if codependency didn't work, let's try the exact opposite!" And there is some logic to that. Sometimes, exact opposites can be very effective. But in this case, the polar opposite, independence, isn't any better. So now, we're going to meet in the middle. A healthy *inter*dependence is needed, in which we recognize that we can't always heal on our own nor should we become overly reliant on a practitioner.

This book will emphasize a healthy interdependence, whereby we can work together and everyone benefits. *Empathipedia* will guide you in how to nurture others but care for them differently from what you have done in the past. What we've been doing has closed down our energy fields, leaving us more susceptible to both our own pain and illness and that of others. This book will show

how you can still use your superpowers and take care of others—but now you'll be able to do so without absorbing their energy and getting sick!

Empathipedia will put the prevention onus on you because, quite simply, no one but you is responsible for preventing your empathic overload and overwhelm. But the book won't leave you hanging. Everything you need to prevent incoming overload is within these pages. This book will guide you, not disempower you.

The disempowerment of the self-help world lies in its healing aspects. While many people have applied the steps in *Self-Care for the Self-Aware* and gotten incredible results, some had more difficulty. That extra difficulty has nothing to do with lack of intelligence, spiritual prowess, or anything the self-critical mind will make up about you; it's more that excessive absorptions of others' energy reduces and blocks our intuition and ability to maintain focus.

More specifically, some readers and people I've worked with have absorbed so much energy over so many years (if not decades!) that to ask them to find specific imbalances is like asking them to look for a needle in a haystack—blindfolded. Obviously, if someone else is there to help you look for said needle, with or without the blindfold, your odds of success are at least doubled.

Empathipedia will explain the importance of creating a safe space with others to help you go deeper. If you read that and thought, "But I want to be able to do this on my own," know that eventually, you will be able to do this on your own, but as with learning a new language, it could take time.

When you work with a quality "space-holder" (someone skilled in holding space for your process), your ability to go deeper within yourself is dramatically increased. One person told me that on average, when safe space is being held, you can go up to 11 times deeper than you can on your own. I'm not sure how she came up with that number—quantifying what can't be quantified? The exact number is irrelevant if it feels right to you that having someone hold safe space for you, or you doing it for them, improves the experience and results. Even if safe space only provides twice as much access, that's still pretty good!

I know some of you are turned off by this mention of teamwork. We HSPs and empaths have learned to isolate ourselves in order to maintain our sense of equilibrium. But to truly heal we have to step into the unknown a bit. I'll share with you safe ways of doing the work. Don't stop here. Please know that I'm only speaking to what I've seen in my practice and what is confirmed via meditations. And more importantly, perhaps, speaking to what makes sense. There are things that work well on a deep level and things that don't. Teamwork helps activate deeper transformations in much less time than solo attempts. When done well, and with the right people, it can even be fun.

Some readers will be able to breeze through this information on their own and easily apply the healing tools and get fantastic results. However, many empaths and HSPs are introverted, or don't feel they have people in their lives who can hold safe space, and I get that. If recruiting others is impossible, reach out to me to be guided through this process. I'm just trying to minimize any chance of you, dear readers, slipping into a downward spiral of self-criticism that often arises from an inability to self-heal to the expected degree. Been there, done that, yes?

In fact, that's been the all-too-common end result of the well-intentioned self-help movement: comparisons and self-criticism. We get upset when we can't master what others tell us we should be able to master. But that's their experience, and perhaps not yours. Let's give ourselves a break. We've been at this for decades, perhaps lifetimes, and to expect to quickly master anything so intense is typically a path to more self-criticism. Let's break that mold now. Let's honor our process.

Invitation

How many half-read or not-yet-opened books are in your home? How many golden nuggets and tools are in those books awaiting your understanding and implementation? Even if you don't resonate with some of the challenges listed in Chapter 3, the A to Z listing, it is highly recommended to read this like a "change-your-life-for-good" book rather than a "fix-your-condition" book. Please read this cover to cover and implement what's here. Not everyone will, but you're not everyone. You are a unique expression of the All—someone who has had more than your fair share of challenges and refuses to give up!

Let this book be a gentle wake-up call that we're all in this together and that we all have similar challenges and goals. Let it be the proverbial knock at the door from the Universe, whose only goal is to see you expand and grow, and who invites you to the next best version of yourself, so that the next time someone calls you "too sensitive" you can say, "Thank you!"

1

Pattern or Truth?

To deeply heal anything, we have to better understand the symptoms and their root causes. If pain and illness are messages, then we need to hear, heed, and work with them. Denying, burying, or eradicating symptoms and their inherent messages with superficial healing or chemicals are typically only temporary fixes.

Just as important as healing work—if not more important—is prevention. We've all gone to practitioners of all types and felt great afterward, but without applying new tools and new ways of being, the symptoms invariably return. Sometimes they reappear very quickly; sometimes it takes years. If you have a back pain, for example, and you do all the things necessary to get you out of pain but don't address the underlying causes, the pain can return in the same or even a different area. If the latter occurs, your practitioner may give it another name and treat you in the same ways that seemed successful the first time. But if those treatments were successful in the deepest possible way the first time, the odds on it returning—in the same spot or elsewhere—would have been dramatically lessened.

One of my clients said she had been successfully treated for lung cancer; years later, however, she had once again been diagnosed with cancer, but this time, in a different area. I shared with her my view that if the original treatment had been more holistic, meaning that if the underlying causes had been addressed in addition to the physical healing work done by her excellent team of well-intentioned doctors, it may not have returned. From a holistic perspective, she had not been fully healed; reoccurrence had only been delayed.

So what were her underlying causes? My medical intuitive reading revealed that she carried an excessive amount of repressed grief. When I mentioned this, she began to cry—a clear sign that I had struck a nerve!

Typically, there are numerous causative layers that need to be uncovered, and ideally, they are worked with one at a time. Each layer has its own story and should be "read" appropriately. Each story has a theme.

The most common theme among the empaths and HSPs I've worked with is Responsibility. A misguided and overblown (even subconscious) sense of responsibility for others is the root cause when someone absorbs unhealthy energies from other people. This overblown sense of responsibility typically began in your more formative years. Some of you literally heard, "It's your responsibility to take care of _____ (fill in the blank)"; others assumed the burden of helping others after noticing an ill (or unhappy) parent or sibling.

If as a result of our acute feelings of responsibility we have the innate sense—or receive the verbalized confirmation—that our actions are received positively, we're more likely to repeat them, and when repeated enough, actions become patterns. As a result of this embedded pattern, as we age we attract others outside the immediate family to whom we feel responsible—friends, romantic partners, work associates, even spouses who know we'll be there for them. If left unhealed, this overdeveloped sense of responsibility can increase to the point that we feel the weight of social issues or even the world on our shoulders.

For any individual who is already highly susceptible to incoming energies, adding unhealthy responsibility is like walking around subconsciously saying, "I'll take your grief" or "I'll take your anger." Because we've not known otherwise, we don't just temporarily feel what's coming our way, we actually embody these energies. And they will stay within us, driving our choices until they are consciously uncovered and healed.

Most, if not all, the people I've worked with are nurturing, caring, sensitive, wonderful, loving, well-intentioned people (well, definitely not one that I can think of—that's a joke). They've received a lot of love or attention or even status for being who they are. They're the ones who others vent to, either in a professional setting or on line at the local grocer. They're the ones others often look up to. They're the ones who always have time, an ear, or an open heart to listen to the trials and tribulations of others.

And none of that is a bad thing, except. . .

The underlying energy of any action is as—if not more— important than the action itself. Meaning, if you are a good listener and are doing so when you'd rather be doing something else, understandably, resentment builds. If you're doing any action from fear, guilt, shame, and especially responsibility, resentment is always the end result because you're not acting in alignment with your truth. Over-responsibility, fear, guilt, shame, and especially resentment close down your energy fields, leaving you more susceptible to your own pain or illness and incoming energies from other people—an energetic sponge.

One of the best practices for determining if you're coming from guilt, fear, shame, or responsibility is to ask yourself, "Pattern or Truth?"

By asking yourself this important question, "Am I coming from my pattern or my truth?" you can begin to shine light upon your unconscious habits. Actions taken as a result of fear, guilt, shame, and especially responsibility create an energetic restriction. Living consciously, mindfully, and with enough practice of presence is the way toward energetic expansion and transformation. Asking "Pattern or truth?" helps us to recognize whether we are being attracted toward an old way of being and to make a new choice in that moment—repeatedly—until the older pattern is overwritten in favor of the newer pattern.

Typically, old patterns can't be energetically cleared or prayed away. They have to be worked with. They need to be noticed and accepted and then integrated as a part of each person's past. This honoring rather than fighting is the starting point toward deep transformation. Too many of us beat ourselves up for decisions we've made in the past that have resulted in patterns not conducive to living in alignment with our higher selves. Is more self-criticism what any of us need? Of course not. We can't punish the self (or others) into being a better person. That's why we need to make friends with our past, recognizing that we did the best we could, given our experience and knowledge at that time. Honoring the past is vitally important. Honoring where we've been is key. When climbing a ladder, do you curse the very rungs you stepped on moments earlier? We need to embrace all of our past, every step along the journey, every rung we stepped on, and every challenge we went through, no matter how painful it was or how deeply it still hurts. Accepting the past creates a better present moment— and by all logical extensions, a better future.

A more tangible comparison is learning a new language. Initially, you start out learning the letters, their sounds, then words, and eventually you can string them together to make full sentences. After a while, oftentimes years, you can be fluent in that language. You may even be able to think in that language. Or have dreams in it. It has become a part of your unconscious mind. We do this all the time. In our formative years, we learn how to relate to people, how to get love, how to give love, when to praise or condemn, when to speak and when to listen. Thoughts, words, and actions—our own and those we've absorbed— have now cemented themselves within us and form the basis of our unconscious belief system. But how many of those are conducive to living a life fully expressed and healthy?

Imagine our negative patterns as having a volume knob that goes from 1 to 10 (queue *Spinal Tap* reference here; you know the one!). There is no zero because nothing can ever be no thing! Our job is to notice when we're at a level 5, and bring it to a 4, then 3, and so on. Similarly, if we're at a 10, our job is to bring it to a

9, then 8, and so on. Thinking we can ever reduce any pattern's attraction—especially a life-long pattern—to a zero is an invitation to misery. Reducing a lifelong pattern to nonexistence is an unrealistic expectation put about by those in denial of the intensity of our past and a misunderstanding of human nature. Moreover, unrealistic expectations often lead to even more self-criticism.

The process of mindfulness and making better decisions is difficult, for sure. But it is the most loving way to make changes because we're embracing the path and every step on it. Deep transformation is never quick. "Feel your buried emotions!" won't sell out a weekend workshop but sometimes, that's what is needed. How many "Heal anything that ails you—FAST" weekend events that don't hold space for emotional release have you already attended? How many books promising rapid health or overnight manifestations have you read and still not gotten yourself to where you want to be? What I'm describing can—and will—take time and effort, but if you really think about it, is anything worth having easily or quickly attained? Please feel into this to determine its truth before judging it.

What We Own Cannot Own Us

People attending Alcoholics Anonymous (AA) meetings introduce themselves by saying, "Hi, I'm _____ (fill in a name), and I'm an alcoholic." In many new age circles, stating what we don't like about ourselves is a no-no. It is believed that giving energy to something you're looking to heal—in this case alcoholism—further cements a person's label and belief that they're an alcoholic.

I see it very differently. I see it as owning and thus diffusing the pull toward drinking alcohol when times are difficult. That pull toward drinking to bury intense emotions may be 10, 30, or 50 years old, but it's still there. By voicing the truth in a room full of people who can relate and won't judge, the energy of the pull is dissipated. In some ways, it's like unloading a secret. Who among us hasn't felt better after voicing something they've been holding onto for too long? If what is said is embraced by others holding what I would call sacred space, the guilt or shame associated with it is reduced. Being seen and heard without judgment, expressing the shadow aspects of self, can be remarkably healing.

When we ask ourselves if we're coming from pattern or truth, we can better elucidate the patterns created by or held in place by guilt, shame, and responsibility. We then illuminate the darkness with love and acceptance, and this creates an opening to a new way of being. Honoring the patterns plagued by darkness brings you closer to the light. Once the past is accepted, we can open to a higher truth by consciously asking: "What is my truth asking of me in this moment? Who or what can I be in this moment that will bring better odds of a more positive outcome for myself and all others involved?"

For example, if your automatic, conditioned reaction to being asked, "Can you make me a sandwich?" is "Of course," ideally, you should determine if that auto-pilot pattern is true. If you've been making a sandwich for someone every day for a few years and would rather not be doing so, you can see how resentment would build. You can see how your throat chakra (one of the seven energy centers in the body, according to Hindu belief) would close down because you haven't yet expressed that you don't want to make that sandwich. When you make a sandwich with a feeling of resentment, you create more blockages that can lead to pain and illness within you. And the sandwich won't taste as good as it would if you were to make it with love!

The first step in asking, "Am I living from my pattern or my truth?" is slowing down. Today's environment is more hectic than ever. It's not uncommon to do several things at once, and at the same time, ironically, thinking that too little is being accomplished. This is the opposite of living a heart-centered, healthy, and connected life. Slowing down, breathing deeply, and asking, "Pattern or Truth?" can give you access to a deeper part of yourself that everyone has but typically isn't recognized or accessed. Becoming deeply immersed in the moment can give you access to your intuitive self, and be the best guide at any time with any person or situation.

Some of the things I've heard people do to help remind them to incorporate "Pattern or truth?" include:

1. **Setting an alarm**. You can set your phone to vibrate every hour and when it does, you can ask this potentially life-changing question.
2. **Notes to self.** You can leave reminder notes all over your home, by your computer screen, on the refrigerator, and so on.

3. **Ring turns**. If you have a diamond ring, for example, whenever the diamond has moved away from the preferred position, as you twist it back to where it belongs you can ask yourself, "Pattern or Truth?"

These are just some of the things I've heard. You can use any or all or make up your own!

When you ask yourself the compelling "Pattern or Truth?" question, if you're calm and centered you'll always be able to intuit the answer. Obviously, if you're stressed or in fear mode, your intuition will likely be reduced or blocked. So, how do you know if you're in your pattern or truth if you're too stressed to intuit a clear answer?

Even Western understandings recognize that we live from our subconscious mind about 80 to 90 percent of the time. I tend to think that it's more than that for most people, but who's counting? It doesn't matter. Odds are high that much of your day-to-day existence and actions are pattern based. How often do you slow down and breathe and take in the present moment? Maybe a few times a day? Maybe a few dozen, or not at all? When you can't intuit the answer, just assume you're operating from your subconscious mind.

Assuming you have determined or even guessed that your patterns are in control and that you're not living your higher truth, you have two options.

Option 1: **Bring yourself to a place of love with a reframe.** In the above example, try on, "How blessed am I that I get to make this sandwich? He does so much for me," and so on. Of course, if you're not feeling that to be your truth, don't lie to yourself. Saying one thing but meaning something else is lacking alignment and integrity and will weaken your energy fields.

Option 2: Speak your truth. This is where the deeper growth and healing happens. We want to be liked and fear we won't be accepted if we state something that can trigger conflict. But as the phrase goes, "Wouldn't you rather be hated for who you are than loved for who you are not?" Truths can be harsh, but if delivered well, our truth is more likely to be received well and will typically be met with respect, even if what you're saying isn't good news to the recipient. Given a choice, would you rather be respected or liked?

Living in alignment with our higher truth is part of what we're here to do. Authenticity and vulnerability can bring us closer to other people.

Not determining and living our truth is what so many of us have already done . . . a lot. And it doesn't work any longer. Similar to learning to ride a bike using training wheels, the training wheels have their purpose until they no longer do. That doesn't make the training wheels bad or wrong; it only makes them a tool we eventually outgrow. Hopefully, with practice and awareness, we can outgrow our past patterns.

Now that you're more aware of the price of not living your truth, you can create new pathways. Ask the big question, answer honestly, then act from this heightened awareness. Answering "Pattern or Truth?" can shift everything.

Living from your higher truth, in alignment with your highest self, can bring about spiritual and emotional growth. It opens you up to connecting with other people in a new, more empowered way. You can be fully present and use your empathic gifts better than ever. Your intuition gets rebooted. Your energy fields expand and your chakras open. A whole new world opens up, and you find yourself being guided to the perfect situations and people with whom you can be your true self.

Does this sound scary? Empowering? Both? It should! Deep growth is why we're here. One of the more common fears associated with this growth is that our friends or intimate partner may not like the new you. To paraphrase Debbie Ford, "Why do we spend so much time getting others to like us? There are already people who don't like us, and we're still fine."

If someone can't hold space for the new you to emerge, or tries to make you feel guilty or small so they can hang onto the old you or maintain their illusion of power over you, you may want to rethink the relationship. This isn't meant to sound mean; rather, it's another opportunity to honor what's authentic for you. Sometimes voicing our deepest selves can increase connection and even inspire others to speak their truth as well. All persons want to be seen and heard for who they really are, so why not express our truth first?

Of course, some may not be inspired by the new you, and that can be okay, too. We can wish them well on their journey, wherever it takes them, at whatever pace that may be. This doesn't make you better than them, only different. They are exactly where they need to be. If a conversation develops with someone you feel you have outgrown, please be patient and loving with your words or you will sound like a pompous gallstone. (Many insults involve calling people by the names of our more loved—and sadly, also shamed—body parts, so I prefer to call people by the names of things we're not big fans of.)

I once had a birthday party in New York City that about 40 of my closest friends attended. We played games, put on a talent show, and had an alcohol-free blast. It was so much fun that a few of us decided to do it again the following year. At the following year's party, someone took me to one side and asked, "Dude, did you get all new friends in the past year?" And when I looked around, about half of them I had met in the last year, and they were all amazing people. Not that the others who weren't invited were bad people; we had just grown in different directions. As you grow, you will attract people more in line with the new you. You will attract those who can see the real you and not be scared, and similarly, you will see and hear where they are at as well. This can create strong bonds of trust and friendship through a co-nurturing, supportive environment. While all this is happening, it's vital not to judge those you've parted from—to do so is judging them and your own past.

Understanding True Responsibility

One of the most powerful insights that ever came through me was, "Metaphysically speaking, no one is responsible for the soul path of another." Whenever I share that I can feel its truth; I can also feel the old pull that says otherwise. That's the pattern in need of transformation!

Taking this awareness out into my own life, I can better see that I'm only responsible for my own soul's path. I can't live other people's lives or lessons for them. If I want to walk the beach with someone, I'd better see two sets of footprints in the sand; it's not my job to carry anyone else's burdens.

Honoring my own path first honors theirs as well. Who am I to think I can or should carry the burdens of others? Does that make any sense at all? Sure, we're all one metaphysically, but physically, we're not, nor should we want to be.

I understand that there are many cultures that believe each person is responsible for healing their lineage. I'm not here to argue with that belief; rather, I am inviting you to decide if that *feels* true for you. Try to get beyond the mind for this one. For many people, trying to heal their lineage has been a life-long pattern, but if that's left you drained, maybe it's not the best use of your energy.

Of course, physical responsibilities must be attended to, such as taking care of your child, or if you're a nurse, taking care of your patients. But those are physical responsibilities that if you don't carry them out, you'll end up in jail or jobless. I'm focusing on a misperception of metaphysical responsibility. Holding onto or trying to process what's not ours to process isn't helping the person whose burden we've taken on. On a soul level, they need what they came here for. Would you want your child, parent, or loved one carrying your burdens? So why would we think they'd want us to do so?

2

The Keyhole Version 2.0

Most empaths are heart centered, and therefore take in life through that chakra. But because of the belief that we need to hold onto energies from others, we close down the back of the heart chakra; we take in energy through the front and keep it. Keeping what's coming your way creates major energetic restrictions that can lead to pain and illness, and of course, leave you more susceptible to keeping what everyone is sending you, unconsciously or not. Typically, we try to prevent this overload via energetic or physical separation.

What are some of the best-known techniques to prevent incoming energies? The technique most people have heard of is to employ some form of "walling," meaning that you create a blockage or separation between you and the difficult person(s) or situation. Specific forms of walling include encapsulating yourself in an energetic bubble, imagining a mirror between you and the difficult person reflecting their energy back to them, or even moving thousands of miles away.

While walling may be a logical method of prevention and may work short term, I compare it to holding up your arms to keep others at bay. How long can you keep up those arms before they get tired? In fact, everyone I've worked with who was suffering from any form of fatigue has been walling off in this way for a really long time. Sadly, walling separates us from the flow of life. On a specific occasion, walling may be the tool you need, but if it becomes the go-to, the repetition forms a new habit. Habitual walling decreasing the chances of receiving intuitive guidance, healing, and vivacity, and it further reduces our ability to truly connect with others. Walling tends to be more fear inspired than the open, welcoming technique of receiving all forms of energy I'm about to share with you.

Welcoming all forms of energy? Why would I want to open to what I don't want?

I understand this concept may sound scary for some of you at first. If you have had a long history of people, or entities, crossing your boundaries, you may want to read through this first and try it only when the timing feels right. And please note: If this frightens you more than it inspires you, please do not attempt this on your own.

Most of us have been taking everything in through the front and keeping it. This creates major energetic restrictions that can lead to pain and illness, and of course, leaves you even more susceptible to keeping what everyone is sending you, consciously or not. Keeping what's coming your way is the bane of the empath's existence!

Walling is a form of fighting what is coming your way, and fighting increases tension, which in turn creates more tension! The Keyhole Version 2.0 works with the flow of life, not against it—even if you judge what's happening as bad or painful.

Opening to all of life may trigger a fear of being energetically overwhelmed. It's important to note, however, that we are (1) opening the chakra, not the heart, and (2) opening both the front and the back of the heart chakra to allow energies to enter, be sifted, then let through and out. We're moving from being a sponge to a funnel while still being able to use our superpower, empathy.

Why not just sidestep incoming energies? Because to do so is to sidestep life. Life itself is always sending us what we need, so it's better to be open to the flow and work with life rather than sidestep—or for that matter, attempt to jump over, or under, or block—what's being sent our way. Having said that, if the sidestep—or for that matter, walling—is what's needed in any moment because opening is too scary or difficult, then use the sidestep or wall until you feel safer to use the Keyhole.

While reading or thinking is a great way to begin to understand a new concept, experiencing something activates more neurons. The more neurons that are fired, the better the chances that a thought will become an embodied reality.

The Keyhole V2.0, described below, gives you more than a one-dimensional, linear understanding by invoking movement, visualization, visceral sensation, vocalization, vibration, sound, and hearing in addition to conceptual awareness.

To get the full effect, especially when starting out, have an arm's length of room on either side of you. Because this will look odd to anyone who doesn't know what you're doing, you may wish to begin when alone. Or in public spaces where it's okay to be different, such as on mass transit.

The Keyhole Process

The Keyhole process is made up of four parts: Steps A, B, C, and D.

Step A: Movement

Expand the heart, and open your arms wide, bringing the shoulder blades back and toward each other. Hold this position for 3 seconds. Now do the reverse: Expand the upper back while bringing the arms forward and contracting the heart space.

Step B: Breath

While expanding the arms and heart space, breathe in and try to feel the air entering the front of the heart chakra. Hold the breath in the center of the body for 3 seconds. Now exhale and expand the upper back while contracting the heart space. Try to feel the air go out the back of the heart chakra.

Step C: Visualization

Imagine energy (in visual art, white is the sum of all colors, so I use a white light) entering the chest on the inward breath while expanding the arms and the heart space. Hold the breath and the image of energy in the center of your heart chakra for 3 seconds. Now exhale and let air and energy exit your body through the rear of the heart chakra as you contract the heart space, while bringing your arms forward, expanding the upper back.

Step D: Vocalization

When you vocalize, you are incorporating voice, opening the throat chakra, feeling vibration in your throat, and hearing your speaking voice as opposed to your inner voice—four activations left dormant when just reading or thinking about something. Repeat the above, expanding the heart and arms, breathing in, imagining energy entering you, and while holding the breath, say out loud, "Keep what's meant for me!" Now do the reverse. At the end of the upper back expansion and after returning the arms to the front, and after breathing and visualizing out the back, say, "Let go of what isn't meant for me!"

Repeat the entire sequence (A, B, C, D) several times until your body feels different.

By using the Keyhole V2.0 you are telling yourself, the Universe, and perhaps your fellow bus riders what you intend to happen. It's a part of manifesting a healthier relationship with energy that lets you be in the flow of life, sift what's incoming, and release what doesn't serve you out the back. I know it sounds simple, but sometimes simple is effective.

When do I do it, and how often?

I suggest doing the above Keyhole V2.0 sequence for 10–15 minutes, two or three times a day—for example, upon awakening, once during the day, and once at night. Dr. Wayne Dyer said that the last five minutes before falling asleep can set up the quality of your night's sleep, so why not tell yourself and the Universe (and your bedmate) what you need to happen while you're most susceptible to incoming energies? And you definitely want to do the Keyhole V2.0 before entering a meeting with a difficult client or any encounter with someone who stresses you, such as, for example, Thanksgiving dinner with your inscrutable Uncle Fred.

What if I forget?

There will be days when you will forget to use the Keyhole, and days when you will have done it less than you wanted to. That's okay. Don't be unrealistic when it comes to mastering something new, even if it makes sense and excites you and is simple; the reality is most of you haven't done this before, and it will take time to incorporate it into daily life. When the Keyhole came to me, I'd not been doing it for over 40 years, so how could I expect to remember to use it all the time? Whenever I realize that I've forgotten, I accept that I've forgotten and just do it then. No self-criticism. No judgments necessary.

What if I can't breathe deeply, or feel more spacey during or after the Keyhole exercise?

Use discretion. Take smaller breaths. Try grounding exercises before beginning. Try holding onto something sturdy with one hand and/or reducing the size of the opening in your heart chakra.

What if I'm in a crowded room, or at a job interview?

There will be times when it seems impossible to do the full range of movements and to use the mantra out loud. Doing the Keyhole V2.0 in your cubicle may incite the boss to call the white-coats. Or if you are the boss, you may want to close the door or excuse yourself to use the washroom (or teach it to your employees!). One of my clients teaches kindergarten and has her pupils do the Keyhole each morning with her. She said that they love it!

If circumstances prohibit you doing the Keyhole, just do a really small version of it—a mini-keyhole! It can be so subtle that no one will know what you're doing. Having done the larger version several times and built your spiritual muscles, you will find that the smaller version will trigger memories of your practice and be just as effective.

How Long Do I Need to Do This? Weeks? Months? Years?

The answer is yes!

If that sounds annoying, frustrating, or angers you—great! I'm happy to trigger those feelings for healing! But seriously, wouldn't you rather have a tool that you know will work every time you use it than not have the tool and always be wondering what to do to protect yourself?

Back to that tooth brushing analogy mentioned earlier, we brush our teeth a few times a day because it's been proven to be effective. The same applies with the Keyhole V2.0. Eventually, you may get to a place where the Keyhole is automatic. Your body and your life experience (not your mind) will show you when you need to do the Keyhole, and at some point will give you the message that you no longer need to.

3

The A–Z of the Most Common
Ailments, Challenges, and Concepts

While the mind will want to (or your fingers already have) jumped to the Healing sections, I want to gently remind you that this book was presented in this order for a reason. The answers you seek may or may not be included in this section, but the information in this section can give you a better understanding of an answer that may arise later in the book or elsewhere in life.

Think of it as a way of gaining momentum as you move toward specific healing work. Each step or concept is designed to give you a better comprehension of what you face, thereby creating a strong foundation for deeper healing when that time occurs.

We're going to take a journey through the symptoms and challenges that we empaths and HSPs tend to face. Of course, not all challenges will be listed here; these are only the most common ones I've worked with. The steps to healing both common and less common symptoms are similar. We have to determine the underlying cause and apply tools to heal those causes at the root, in addition to making the needed lifestyle changes to prevent reoccurrence. The healing tools are detailed in Chapters 4, 5, and 6, but as noted above, it's best to read through this section before skipping ahead.

Abandonment

Underneath it all—under the fears of losing your family members or intimate partner, the fear of losing your home, your health, or financial assets—is the dreadful grief each of us experienced in that first moment we felt separate from Source.

Prior to incarnating into our present corporeal form, each of us was pure energy in a vast soup of even more energy, which I call Source. We each felt supported and loved unconditionally. Then, one day, we decided to join the physical world. We chose our human family to be born into as the perfect scenario for us to experience what we needed to experience based on our karma, which doesn't care if what we're incarnating into is good or bad by human standards. All experiences are part of a jigsaw puzzle that includes all aspects of humanity. For us to ascend, we need to experience all of them. All. Of. Them.

But few pains we experience later in life come near the level of pain we feel as a result of what I call our original sin ("sin" meaning misperception rather than breaking a rule). This original sin is the misperception that we are separate from Source, the only experience of unconditional love we've ever known. Not that we are separate; it just feels that way based on our physical senses, which begin to dominate experience as we grow from infant to young child.

The moment when we realize the separation varies for each of us, but I sense that for most it happens when the umbilical cord is cut at birth, separating us from our mother, followed by the formation of what feels like a painful void in the solar plexus as a result of that separation. This void is the lack of unconditional love made manifest.

The heart-wrenching agony of perceived separation forms our first feelings of abandonment, which few of us want to acknowledge, much less face and heal. And what we don't acknowledge will repeat until we face it and heal it.

Imagine, for example, that your intimate partner has left you or your loved one has passed over. While that in itself is painful enough, it has also triggered the unhealed pain from the original sin. The fear of feeling that pain leads us to form unhealthy attachments to feelings, experiences, people (codependency), and possessions—unconscious attempts to avoid grieving our original separation from Source.

We close ourselves off from feeling that pain by creating what I perceive as numerous super-thin layers of protection around the heart, like a multi-layered metaphysical pericardium. But with each attempt to not feel the pain, we also create walls that increase the sense of separation and minimize our ability to give, receive, or feel love. So part of our job here is to recognize and acknowledge the fear of abandonment that subconsciously runs most of our lives, then heal it!

We are here to heal each layer of protection in order to better access the heart's wisdom and abilities. But those layers don't break easily. And when they crack a little bit, even though more heart energy is available, the fear of losing our protection and feeling the original sin once again is too great for most of us to manage, much less consciously step into.

When we feel our heart is breaking, what is really happening is that each protective layer is cracking, and by allowing those layers to break, we can finally regain the connection to Source that we are all seeking but too easily forget or distract ourselves from. And distraction is our specialty. We spend most of our lives trying to fill the void left by the original separation with things that don't actually fill the void but rather, temporarily mask its existence. Higher-quality spiritual growth and healing work has to stay aware of this distinction. To truly heal this void, we need to stay aware of this distraction game and heal it at the root level.

Healing this void is done by recognizing its existence and loving it. The tools and concepts in *Empathipedia* will help you on this journey.

Abundance

Who wouldn't like to be more abundant? For a while, I didn't. I thought money wasn't spiritual. As you can probably guess, I was broke.

Eventually, I got past the misperception that money wasn't spiritual and instead misinterpreted other spiritual teachings, believing that if only I could be awesome the Universe would provide financial support, that I didn't have to focus on or even think about money. I quit a relatively cushy job to find myself, and after a year of searching, all I found was myself deep in debt!

Moral: Don't be a Dave. Or at least not *that* Dave!

We all have innate gifts, talents, and skills. Many of us learn additional skills from individuals or institutions. If we focus on giving, sharing, or selling our gifts, talents, or services to those who need them, one would assume that abundance would follow, right? But even that is too simplistic. What is our energy under the giving? What is the recipient's energy? Is there an unrealistic expectation or an attachment to an outcome by either or all parties involved? And perhaps more importantly, what are our true beliefs about money, and where did those beliefs come from?

If the giving of a gift or the sharing of a skill is done from a place of responsibility, guilt, fear, shame, or worse, pity, the energy under the giving will feel constrictive. If whatever is done is performed from love or true compassion, it will feel constructive.

For example, thoughts like *What will they think of me?* or *What will I think of myself if I don't do what they're asking* are more fear-based than love-based. If we make a habit of constrictive transactions, we may find ourselves feeling resentful. Fear and resentment negatively affect our energy flow, leading to blockages that don't let us express our truest selves nor attain—or co-create opportunities for—a heart-centered sense of financial freedom. If we find ourselves continually asking where our reward is, just the fact that we are asking should tell us that the giving is more constrictive than constructive. That could be an indication that even our charitable gifting is more egocentric than our mind has convinced us it is.

Constructive transactions that include money or barter for goods and services performed with realistic expectations, transparency, and integrity will always feel better to all parties involved. Instead of the resentment that builds with constrictive giving, constructive giving, sharing, or selling will keep our energy fields open and flowing, a precursor to better health and vivacity.

Obviously, more inner flow can lead to increased and mutually beneficial energetic and physical exchanges and therefore, a sense of abundance. Highly Sensitive Persons thrive in these types of transactions. We don't want to take advantage of others, nor do we want to be taken advantage of (I know, no one does), so we're best suited to seeking more magnanimous pursuits. Empaths often want to share their heart-centered skills as an occupation. Others, not quite in their dream job yet can challenge themselves to bring a higher awareness to any occupation and find the beauty within that opportunity. Either path incorporates a heart-centered knowing that abundance can follow a gracious inner state, rather than seeking abundance first.

Seeking abundance that does not incorporate the heart often includes fear-based decisions that typically augment the fear. Rather than a specific number in a bank account, our definitions of abundance include an emotional aspect of doing, being, and sharing that leads to a sense of wholeness. That said, we shouldn't limit our options. If we show the Universe that we understand the value of money and use it for the betterment of all, there is more chance we'll be sent more opportunities to make larger amounts of money.

Another blockage to financial abundance is our neuro-association about money that often goes back to how we perceived money being used in childhood. Some parents bought things for their children as a way of connecting with their child or as a reward for being "good." Though well intentioned, these gestures were often inclusive of attachments to a way of being or an end result. If money was given or withheld due to our behaviors, it taught us which actions were deemed positive or negative. Money was a control mechanism and the energy by which power—or love—was either given or taken away.

I worked with a woman recently who asked me about her lack of abundance. I intuited to say, "To you, money equals power. Because your dad was a powerful man and used his power and money in ways you don't perceive as loving, your belief is that money isn't loving."

She felt the truth of that, and I intuited for her to visualize her dad and say, "I love you, but I don't want to be like you." She repeated this phrase numerous times until the mantra went from just a thing to say to really feeling it in the heart. Tears flowed.

Now that we were in that softened heart space, I intuited to have her imagine herself sharing her gifts and receiving money for that. She described the scenes in her mind to me, detailing what she'd be doing and how the giving of her gifts would be received. All was beautiful and flowing until a layer of resistance arose.

To me, resistance is a detour sign, not a stop sign, that reveals what needs to be addressed next. At this point, I intuited the next layer in her abundance blockage was her fear of being more successful than her dad. Thoughts of her outearning him, she believed, would increase his anger and deepen their separation from each other, and no child wants their parent to be mad at them!

So we did another visualization of her talking with her dad's Higher Self. While still in the softened heart, we asked him if he'd be angry or proud if she became more abundant than he was. More tears were released as his Higher Self wished her well and supported her success. She looked 20 pounds lighter when we were done.

As you can see, there are often multiple causal layers of our blockages. And many of the deeper layers can't be seen until the more superficial layers are healed. In many cases, we're looking to reverse decades of thinking—typically others' beliefs that we've adopted. Our beliefs about some subjects, money for example, can be extra difficult to heal because there are often numerous deeply engrained ideologies that have to be excavated and consciously worked with.

Someone asked me how I got rid of my insecurity about sharing my gifts, especially lacking formal letters after my name. I responded with, "Who says I got over my insecurity?" Rather, when I hear that silly little voice, I embrace it as part of the journey. I recognize insecurity is as much a part of me as any security might be. And I bless it. I then center myself and ask my Higher Self, "What can I do or be in response to what exists?"

When I focus on that, the answers come. Writing this book, for example, is one thing I've been hearing clearly. If I focus only on paychecks from the publisher, answers will come in alignment with the fear-based belief of lack. When I remember that each chapter or even one sentence has the potential of catalyzing a new way of being for a reader looking for answers, I get excited to continue writing!

Within that excitement is gratitude for the opportunity to share my gift, and I trust that this expression of energy is met with a return of energy, either financial or otherwise. When I see people suffering and ask what I can do about it, I intuit to share my gifts, whether it's via a private session or group experience, this book or even another book by another author, or just quite simply being nice to a stranger.

And I always intuit things that I know I can do. I never hear, "Create a formula to open up the fabric of the space-time continuum to make time travel accessible. Only then will you be abundant beyond belief." As much as I'd like to invent said formula, I'm probably not the person who is going to do that.

While it's healthy and necessary to grow and challenge ourselves, some challenges are too far beyond our personal abilities but are easy for another person or organization (well, maybe not the time- and space-travel wormhole). I can support other persons and organizations in ways I feel called to, though—for example, by donation or by sharing their mission with others—because we are here to heal the hurt through whatever means we have or can attain.

We should all do what we can with what we've been given, but beyond that we should think twice. How many of you have brought on your own anxiousness by focusing on or fearing things beyond your control? If everyone followed their guidance and did what they are here to do, don't you think the world would be a much better place? And in regards to the original subject, wouldn't you feel more abundant getting paid for using those gifts rather than trying to create what's not yours to create?

Empaths and HSPs typically understand that money and even goods and services are forms of energy. And we know that uneven exchanges of energy are constrictive. If we're feeling underpaid and/or underappreciated in our day job, that doesn't mean the day job is bad; it means we've co-created an opportunity to experience a constrictive aspect of ourselves that no longer fits. So we can either change our attitude about our day job or seek or create a new opportunity. But if the latter is done without healing the wound of feeling underappreciated, the wounds eventually resurface.

The constriction associated with underappreciation is an internal game. If we believe in ourselves and are grateful for what does exist, even if it's not the perfect job for us at a given time, we're more apt to receive higher-quality guidance for creating our next opportunity.

I've met many amazing, loving, caring, and nurturing people who have remarkable gifts to share but lack either the groundedness or the skillset for self-employment. In these situations, the security derived from working a day job can offer a strong foundation for spiritual and emotional growth and healing during hours outside of work. If we're open to growing, we'll be sent the perfect situations and persons to trigger unhealed wounds within us. Employers or fellow employees can be as much of a source for triggering our own wounds as our intimate partners. We should make the most of whatever opportunity is in front of us.

Even if you're convinced you should be elsewhere, there is often a chance for some kind of healing to commence in your current position.

If we listen to our Higher Selves, we will always know what to do or be in response to what exists, and that includes where and how best to share our gifts. Focus on those, and abundance will follow.

Acceptance

The concept of acceptance took me two years to understand! (Yes, I can be a bit stubborn at times.) No one could explain it to me in a way that made any sense. All I could think was, "Why would I want to accept what I don't want?"

Being a former editor, what helped me was following the word "acceptance" with an ellipsis (. . .) not a period. Meaning, I can accept what exists *and* still do something about it. "Acceptance" followed by a period indicated to me that any condition or experience was final, and therefore, there was nothing I could do to change it.

What I later understood was that energetically, fighting what exists adds to the fight. Clearly, that's not my desired process or outcome. Accepting what already exists allows me to ask what can be done from that more centered place. This is more conducive to experiencing what we wish to experience, or at minimum, reducing the draining and often futile fight against what obviously already exists. It's a subtle paradigm shift in understanding that can have powerful effects.

I once heard Marianne Williamson speak about her experience of asking people to sign her peace petition. After too few showed interest, she yelled out (and I'm paraphrasing), "WHY ISN'T ANYONE SIGNING MY GODDAMN PEACE PETITION?" In that moment, she realized that she wasn't being the change she wished to see. She took ownership and recognized that her energy was turning people away. Of course, at our core, everyone wants peace. And those who don't, need it more than anyone else.

> *Whatever the present moment contains, accept it as if you had chosen it. Accept—then act. Always work with it, not against it. Make the present your friend and ally, not your opponent. This will miraculously transform your whole life.*
>
> —Eckhart Tolle, Author

Alcohol

After I've shared with them the story of getting drunk without drinking alcohol, many empaths and HSPs have told me they too can get drunk just by being around other people who are drinking. HSPs might want to rethink any inclinations to stay all night at the local bar. Oftentimes, the energies you might absorb are the emotional pains of the fellow patrons. The exposure to and accumulation of any of that negative energy can alter your own energy body and eventually affect your physiology in line with the commonly understood effects of drinking alcohol.

For many empaths and HSPs, empathically transmitted drunk vibes are many times worse because we may not be aware that the pain we're feeling isn't our own. It just feels like more pain. More pain is often more incentive to bury the pain via more consumption of alcohol. This is a dangerous cycle.

If I sound judgmental, that's not my intention. I've been there; I too have drunk alcohol and at the time justified doing so. I got several wakeup calls and never answered the phone, until the one time (well, actually, twice) I almost paid the ultimate price. My hope is that you learn from my mistakes or answer your own wakeup calls from something higher than ourselves. Escaping our pain with any foreign substance further buries the causative energies, delaying healing and worsening symptoms.

Ask yourself what, if anything, are you trying to escape and can it be addressed in a more constructive way? Or perform the Body Scan exercise found later in this book to discern if that pain you're feeling is even yours!

Some empaths and HSPs who drink alcohol may say, "It's only a couple of drinks" or "I only drink a few times a year." For them, perhaps, alcohol consumption isn't a major issue. But for those who drink more often and/or more alcohol per sitting, let me offer a gentle reminder (which you already know is true but may not want to be reminded of): If you continue to drink, it likely will affect you in harmful and increasingly insidious ways.

The world needs you present, here and now. Your higher self is always calling you to a higher vision of yourself, and alcohol consumption poisons your awareness of your calling or your ability to follow it. If divinity lives within, then why poison her home?

Anger

I once worked with a woman who on the outside projected an image of someone who'd done her work, was very loving, and who could share her gifts of connection quite often. But upon getting to know her, I saw that only two of those were true. She hadn't done her work. She buried her anger from her childhood under big juicy hugs and words that calmed the anxious minds of others. She hugged everyone who came within her presence. Like "The Hugging Saint" Amma, her pudgy, motherly, physical and energy bodies radiated enough goodness you couldn't help but lose yourself in her arms.

I was a bit surprised that when it came time for us to do a session, she spoke about chronic and painful muscle tightness. I intuited she was holding a lot of anger and shared this with her.

She looked at me, tilted her head leftward a bit, and softly said, "Oh, I don't do anger."

I replied, "I agree. You don't do anger; it's doing you."

People come to me to tell them the truth of what I see, sense, or hear. I don't find value in excessive sugarcoating unless "instructed" to do so. As a practitioner, we have to be cognizant of what people need to hear, and how best to deliver it. Sometimes, the shock value of the above response and others like it is necessary to snap someone out of complacency. Sometimes it's taken well; other times, not so much. But truth has a way of finding us, whether we like what we're hearing or not . . . including that we all have anger.

Anger burial and/or denial is quite common with many people I work with. We've experienced our share of anger already, usually directed at us in painful ways. Knowing how that felt, we swore we'd never direct our anger toward others. So whatever anger we had, we buried. And, in a subconscious effort to reduce anger in others, we absorbed and held onto their anger as well. We were (and often still are) under the illusion that if we could do this enough, not only would that other person feel better but we'd feel safer, too. The mind thinks, "If I can heal this person, even by being a sponge for their anger, they'd be less likely to attack me."

So we learned absorption as a method to stay safe. But this only works temporarily. Over time, empathically transmitted anger creates enough stagnation that muscles can tighten, blood pressure can rise, and we can assume a heightened and prolonged state of fight, flight, or freeze. The sympathetic nervous system (SNS) does a great job of keeping us safe in perilous situations, but overuse of the SNS retrains the body to live in that heightened state more frequently. For some people, it becomes constant—muscles tighten with such ferocity they don't want to release, and raised blood pressure over time may develop into the new norm. You can take muscle relaxants, of course, but that doesn't address the root cause. Similarly, blood pressure medication treats the symptoms but doesn't address the cause. If you need the medication, you should use it, but you should be aware of what the medication is and isn't doing.

No one likes being angry. Maybe a few seem to thrive on it, but unprocessed anger can't be healthy over the long run. Eventually, people who bury their anger are smacked down by the proverbial two-by-four and forced to face their demons. Some will face those demons, some won't. Some will in this lifetime, and others will wait till the next go 'round.

If you already know you're angry, or if after doing the Body Scan, as described in Chapter 4, you have discovered repressed anger, seek help. Work to heal it; otherwise, it will eat you up from the inside out. Anger will cloud all your decisions. It will keep your heart guarded, push love away from you, and minimize your ability to receive any love headed your way. Repressed anger can destroy your life, but fighting it only makes it worse.

Anger is a normal part of human existence. It can even be a catalyst for great change. It doesn't define you, but it is a part of you. You cannot thrive without it any more than you can thrive without love. But it doesn't have to own you—meaning, anger doesn't have to color all of your choices; with work, you can own it rather than it owning you.

Shadow energies must be honored, not pushed away. The aforementioned woman didn't want to own up to having any anger, so there wasn't a lot I could do for her. Although I enjoy working with skeptics, it's difficult to help someone who isn't open to what's being exposed. Having anger doesn't make you a bad person; it makes you quite human. Even the current Dalai Lama laughed when asked if he gets angry and then said, "Of course I do; I'm human." It's more about *what you do* with the anger than *if* you have any.

Anxiet-me

When stressed, the mind will try to control things, people, and situations to attain mental equilibrium. To paraphrase Buddhist teacher Pema Chödrön, the mind is always seeking certainty in an inherently insecure world. Fear of uncertainty leads to anxiousness.

The mind may then say, "If I can figure out why I feel anxious, then I can heal it" and at first will look anywhere but within for that appeasement. Some people try meditation, but they never seem to get to a place where they drop their thoughts, and this creates even more anxiousness!

I think if the mind had an "off" switch, we'd all have worn it out by now. Fighting the ever-present thought process or looking for ways to escape it hasn't worked yet. And our judgments about having an overactive mind make the process even more difficult.

Because we've been taught to judge so many parts of ourselves, emotions included, the mind will do its best to minimize our feelings. It will rationalize, bury, or even deny raw human emotions just to attain and hopefully maintain some sort of steadiness—to look like we've got everything under control. But we don't. The tension between what exists and what we wish would or wouldn't exist creates what Western medicine calls Anxiety. But we're more than a diagnosis.

Because the power to manage the tension is within us, let's call this, Anxiet-me.

In my own life, I know that whenever I notice myself being anxious, snippy, or crabby, it is because I haven't managed my emotions or incoming energies well. Rather than get too caught up in that crabbiness, I do my best to catch myself and work with it in the moment. If I find my mind blaming others, insulting people, wishing things or relationships were different, complaining, and so on, it serves as a signal of my lack of acceptance of a given situation or person.

On the rare occasions when I've not caught the signal in time, my vision is actually affected. People or things that used to look great lose their beauty for me. It's an odd yet effective wakeup call that something within me is off. I use this as a reminder to do my work. And if I'm really crabby for too long, my wife will call me on it (lovingly) and hold the space needed for me to process my chaotic internal state.

Typically, any sense of anxiety-me within us activates the mind's desire to distract from what is present. The mind then takes us on an un-merry-go-round of blaming others for what we feel. It's easy and convenient to place the blame outside oneself, but while blaming others is enticing to the ego, it is ultimately disempowering to the self. Blaming other people for our discomfort denotes a lack of self-awareness, and operating from heightened emotions rather than self-awareness typically leads to even more pain. Other people are just doing what they're doing and being who they're being within the realm of what they know.

We empaths and HSPs have the burden of carrying others' anxiousness and stress in addition to our own, so even after we've done a ton of inner work, we may still have the uneasy feeling that we've missed something. And we *have* missed it. Anxiet-me is insidious. It is typically very difficult to find, but once found it can be healed.

One of the most powerful ways to heal anxiousness is also the most challenging (sorry, I don't make the rules; I just intuit them): we must access the emotional and energetic body. As we know, resistance to what exists only creates more resistance, so we must make a conscious effort to slow down and open to what's there, even if it is uncomfortable.

Once our attention is focused inward—ideally while being held in safe space—it's easier to determine if this anxiousness is yours or another's that you've absorbed empathically. If what we're experiencing belongs to someone else (anxiousness), we have to give it back. If it's ours, we have to own it so that it doesn't own us. Those steps will be detailed in Chapters 5 and 6.

Ascension

Sure, it's fun to channel Melchizedek from the 13th dimension. It can also be enjoyable pursuing 5D consciousness or enlightenment. Outer realm communication can be inspiring, educational, and even calming, but if these pursuits are distracting from the 3D, linear, existent world, your attention won't be here now, in the body. As the vehicle for the soul and a receptacle for intuition, the body is a gift that shouldn't be minimized or ignored, nor is it wise to try to escape the body, even if we're in pain. Another way to look at this is, if Source is within you, keep your inner home clean and hospitable for Source to inform and guide you. To paraphrase author Jeff Brown, "Ascend with both feet on the ground."

I've seen the results of ungrounded spirituality in countless clients who are wonderful, caring, loving people. They only want to do the work they came here to do, but by pursuing more esoteric studies without taking care of their bodies, their pain and illness only worsened. If they had had more body awareness, they might have worked directly with their minor aches and pains before those blockages worsened, acknowledging their pain as a message that something they were doing was out of alignment with their higher path.

Many people buried their symptoms with artificial substances. Many thought they'd healed what was there because they'd received some medications, supplements, or energy work and the symptoms went away. While that is possible, if the underlying causes weren't addressed, it's more likely the symptoms will return days or years later, and with more intensity. Still others tried to escape their pain by studying metaphysics, quantum physics, channeling, aura readings, and so on. If those are your passions, great! But if they're done to minimize or escape what your body has been telling you, well, not so great. Ironically, trying to heal the symptoms in this way can leave you in physical pain, depressed, or lethargic—or all three!

I read that a channeled ascended master said that ascension means to rise above the fate of your past, indicating that ascension isn't solely evolving beyond form. If you really think about it, by its very nature, focusing on an ascension is not being in the present. Though I see the attraction, living for the future isn't any better than reliving the past. We can't change the past, and though I'm open to being wrong, we can't rush enlightenment, either. I feel our growth goals should be more day to day. That doesn't mean we should not have any plans for the future; rather, I'm inviting you to consider the possibility that creating the best present-moment experience will lead to better future experiences, too.

By handling and healing what arises in the now, we can live more in alignment with what our highest self wants for us. In my experience, those claiming "to escape the duality" (AKA being overly persistent in seeking oneness) that is inherent in human existence are really looking to escape their pain. And while I'm all for healing, growing, and expanding ourselves, running away from our pain or escaping our earthly existence is not the method that is most effective. Instead, we should embrace whatever arises in the body in the present moment and work to heal it with love, compassion, and the proper tools.

Awakening

In your mind's eye, imagine the collective unconscious of everyone who is alive today. What does that look and feel like? Probably not very good, right? The collective anxiety and grief are approaching levels most would call unbearable. The divisiveness and subsequent anger is perhaps at an all-time high in our present lifetime.

You are that.

Huh? What does that mean?

What I mean is that we are connected to and a part of the collective unconscious at all times; the empath and HSP just happen to feel these energies to a higher degree. We are affected by what's happening outside us, and what's happening internally is also affecting what's outside us. We find it difficult to act upon this awareness in a consistent way because our physical senses aren't tuned in to the collective unconscious, but we are always affected and affecting.

Let's try an exercise.

Invite an awareness of the collective unconscious to come to you. Let it take however long it needs, and try not to fear what is already a part of you. The image and the feelings may be difficult to stay with, but do your best.

Now send yourself self-love. Embrace any aspect of you that you've disliked. It can be physical (your nose, for example); it can be emotional (your anger, for example); or it can be an event you've been unable to forgive yourself for. Stay with this image and feeling. Keep loving it and yourself.

What is happening to the collective unconscious when you do that?

Most of us who try this find that the collective unconscious follows our thoughts and feelings about ourselves. Even though our part in the collective unconscious is tiny at best, our iota of self affects all of us and everything.

So all we have to do is stay open and loving to awaken all of humanity? No pressure, Dave. Thanks for nothing.

Wouldn't it be nice to always be open and loving and have that awaken humanity? While it might be awesome, the statement is only partially true. We do have to do our part. And if we focus on healing humanity first, without also doing our individual work, it's going to be a much more difficult endeavor; instead, we must acknowledge that humanity is an outward reflection of our inner experience.

Our responsibility for awakening humanity begins, ironically, when we remember that we must take care of our individual selves first and that anything we do affects the whole. If humanity is feeling lots of anxiety, we need to do our inner work to stay centered. We don't have to absorb what's coming our way and hold onto it. When we have a calm inner core, we're more open to guidance on how we can best affect what's inside and outside of ourselves.

Sounds great, but how can I minimize or eliminate the effects of the collective unconscious upon my individual self?

We have to take active steps to be a part of the collective unconscious but also apart from it. Because we are constantly bombarded with external energies, we have to remain vigilant in allowing what's not ours to flow through us rather than absorb it. If you're feeling anxious, tense, scared, sad or even sick for what seems like no immediate reason, it could be that you're picking up toxic energies from the collective.

The open, flowing state required in order for us not to be affected by the collective unconscious isn't our usual state, so consistent effort is needed to get there and stay there. We need to allow ourselves to remember and forget things on a regular basis and activate inner calm and galvanize an open flow. The tools for making this happen are asking, "Pattern or Truth?" and the Keyhole Version 2.0 that are detailed in Chapters 1 and 2. As with any habit-forming process, the more we do it the quicker our brains will rewire to support this new way of being.

Benefits

So many of us have been told that our sensitivities make us weak, or that we're not attractive when we cry, or any number of other myths that make sensitivity seem like a curse. We hear these things repeatedly and are told to toughen up. We don't feel accepted by those who are closest to us and those who we feel should love us unconditionally. We therefore don't accept ourselves and continue these self-critical thoughts until we realize that's not helpful and begin to do our inner work. When we realize that sensitive is how we are, we want to express even more of what we've been taught to repress. But society and even our self-judgment are always there trying to keep us small.

That is society's issue, not ours. If others can't accept us for who we are, that's a reflection of their own inability to accept themselves or even life itself. It's not easy, but we have to work to free ourselves of the bondage that comes from believing everyone else's lies about who we are and how they think we should be.

So, what are the benefits of being sensitive? Isn't it easier to just be normal?

If normal means closed-hearted, unexpressive, and unable to give and receive deep love, count me out! We are normal—atypical for sure, but still normal. Normal to me means human with all the characteristics that go with that experience. Shutting down is common but also unhealthy and never works in the long term.

We're here to experience all aspects of self, and those who befriend their sensitivity can do so.

Yes, we feel a lot, and it's not always comfortable. In fact, oftentimes it's painful. But by being aware of and healing energies we have empathically absorbed from those closest to us and the collective unconscious, we can use our sensitivities appropriately, and see them as the gift they were meant to be. We can feel what's going on with others and respond in kind. We can know how to respond with a compassionate ear or heart to any situation. We can always know if others need empathy or empowerment. Awareness of pain and suffering activates more incentive to heal it. We are here to spread love.

It's okay to feel everything. It's unhealthy, however, to keep everything that is being sent our way. Given a choice to feel deep and profound love rather than living an insular existence, wouldn't you choose the former? The flip side, of course, is the ability to feel deep heartache. This is the human experience. Living small or unemotional is not what we came here for. By applying the tools in this book, we can use our gifts for the betterment of all and ride the waves of emotion like a roller-coaster.

Who else can heal the hurt but those who can truly feel it? Who else can know on a deeper level what's going on with the world and how to heal that, too? Not that healing the world is our responsibility; rather, consider doing your part along with all the other healers and way-showers. We get to show others that while pain may be inevitable, suffering isn't. We can feel what's true beyond the layers of the mind, where we sense our part in waking up the collective humanity, one person at a time—beginning with ourselves!

Boundaries

You know how in some countries it's normal to stand really close to another person and in other countries it's more common to stand a few feet away? Empaths and HSPs can feel like we're inside the bodies of other people, whether they're two feet away or twenty. Our physical body desires space, but our energy body wants to merge. If the desire to merge is coming from a learned pattern of how to connect based on fear of not being liked, we'll contort our thoughts, words, and actions to get that approval. We'll do or say anything to avoid rocking the proverbial boat, including acquiescing to the needs of others. We people-please because we believe that if we do, things will go smoothly. I call this, Borderless Personality Disorder.

This version of BPD includes enmeshment and codependency. We become walking sponges, taking on the characteristics of others around us like a chameleon. But we take on more than just colors; we absorb the energy of others in order to resonate with them. The mind believes that by resonating with someone, we'll be safer. And that may be true to a point. But as with many things that are good in small doses, they can be quite harmful if overdone.

The following exercise involves both of your hands and may be difficult to do if you're holding this book, so if possible, have someone read it to you. If you're on your own, see if you can prop this book up so that you can read and do what's instructed. You'll get a lot more "wow!" by freeing both hands and doing what's recommended.

BPD Exercise

Place your hands about 12 inches apart, at the level of the heart chakra, palms facing inward toward the opposite palm. The left hand represents you, the right hand represents another person.

Slowly move the palms toward each other, and interlock the fingers. Now lower the head a bit and angle the clenched hands, thumbs toward your sternum, so that your face is facing your knuckles. Now wiggle all of your fingers.

Notice that, at first glance, without consciously thinking that a particular hand is facing a particular direction and therefore the fingers are facing left or right as well, that it's difficult to determine which hand's fingers are facing any direction. These "lost in the other" fingers are a representation of codependency.

Now return the hands to the original position. Once again, you are the left hand, and the right hand represents someone else. Slowly bring each hand toward the other, palms facing inward. Now, instead of interlocking your fingers, gently touch all of your fingertips with the corresponding fingertips of the other hand. Then allow the palms to touch each other.

Once again lower the head a bit and angle the gently touching hands toward your face.

What position is this? Some call it prayer position. Others call it *namaste*. The Indian Hindu word *namaste*, familiar to many people from yoga practice, means "the beauty within me sees and honors the beauty within you." There is no enmeshment, only acknowledgment that you are connecting with another person from a place of clarity. You are meeting them without unhealthily merging with them.

In this prayer position, you don't need anything from another person. You are separate but also together. This is a representation of a healthy boundary. Whether you touch someone physically or not, honoring their "being" from a place of your "being," without needing anything from them, is unconditional acceptance made manifest. From this point of view, we are truly free and never alone. The boundaries between you and others are clearer and the energetic transmission between you can be worked with to fully honor what's true for you and for them.

Clothing

A fair number of empaths and HSPS have said they're sensitive to tight clothing and also to certain types of fabrics. Clothing contains the energies of the materials themselves and any chemicals added, for example pesticides in the case of cotton. The lack of breathability in some fabrics creates an almost claustrophobic reaction in some HSPs. Also found within clothing is the energy of those who design, make, distribute, and sell it and the energies of all the persons cultivating the basic materials.

Considering how much of what we wear contains dyes, unnatural materials, and the greed inherent within the every-season-every-year-a-new-style consumerism, this is not a good match for an HSP! Our skin is a lot more permeable than we like to think. Toxic chemicals can make their way into your pores and cause allergic reactions/detoxification symptoms. Choose organic, natural fiber clothing whenever possible.

Compassion

Only hurt people hurt people. The sentence is a bit of a mantra for me. Whenever I see, or read or hear about someone hurting another person, my initial reaction is often cringing. I close up. But eventually, whether it takes seconds or days, I remember the mantra: only hurt people hurt people. I can then open up again and practice compassion.

It's easier to open up knowing that those you see doing harm to other people, animals, and the planet aren't bad people per se; they are hurting inside. Typically, they don't have the tools to manage the emotional pain. They've built a suit of armor around their tender hearts in an attempt to protect those hearts from further hurt. Sadly, this closing down creates even more pain. Some people who have been hurt will unconsciously hurt others in an attempt to get back the power they perceive someone has taken from them, even if the causative event happened decades prior. While initially it may not be easy to have compassion for someone expressing intense levels of unprocessed emotional pain by inflicting more pain on others, perhaps this mantra can slowly begin to cultivate compassion leading to healing.

Why would you have compassion for those who are hurting others? Isn't it easier to call them some kind of monster, seek "justice" (justified revenge), or want to hurt them back? Or at minimum, try to get that person locked up?

While those are common questions and understandable reactions, it's not the heart-centered choice, the only choice that truly heals. Throwing someone in prison without rehabilitative therapy only further buries the causative energies, almost assuring that if or when they get out, they're even more likely to commit another crime. Perhaps they were abused and never experienced love. Perhaps their default settings now are "hurt or be hurt." Maybe they were the childhood bully or as an adult sought power through money or rank.

True compassion can heal the hardest of hearts. For a person in pain, it can fill a need, and if someone has an unfulfilled need and we can provide that, why wouldn't we? Saying that they're not deserving of compassion based on their unconscious reactions to their past can feed the fires within them. And it's highly judgmental of us to think that someone isn't deserving of love. Given a particular set of conditions, who's to say that we wouldn't act in a similar manner?

I saw an interview with someone whose occupation was to torture political prisoners. As emotionally painful as it was initially to see that such a vocation exists, it was equally painful to hear that he enjoyed his work. I had to ask myself, *What could have happened in this person's life to close his heart so much that his only method of release was to hurt others?*

Who among us has ever looked into the eyes of a newborn and said, "Oh, yeah, there's some evil right there."? No one is born evil.

No one is born judgmental. No one is born a criminal or racist or a homophobe.

Babies are victims of all of the energies around them in addition to direct learnings, and sometimes, they're victims of abuse. Children are easy targets for those adults with unresolved emotional conflicts. To begin healing the hurt, we need to minimize and eventually eliminate the cultural, societal, national, or even religious indoctrinations of separatism and better than/less than ideologies that propagate the pain and minimize the heart's inherent compassion.

If we've been victims of less than compassionate teachings and upbringings, it's up to us to give ourselves now what we wish had been given to us then. Self-compassion is one of the best gifts we can give ourselves. And you'll notice that the more you are nice to yourself, the more others are too.

If you hurt others in the past, apologize when possible and promise to them that you've learned what not to do. If a direct apology isn't possible, ask Spirit to send them your message. But mean it. A casual prayer is no better than a casual apology. Feel the pain you've inflicted on others within you. Then choose self-compassion to heal the wound that made you act out an unconscious pattern. The deeper this is done, the more likely that wound will heal, assuring you do not repeat the pattern.

No matter what others have done, think about being compassionate the next time you see them. Feel deeper into your own body when imagining yourself being open and loving and understanding of their situation. How does it feel? Even if you're really angry, work through that by challenging yourself to imagine what I'm saying here—that no one is born evil.

What is the visceral sensation? Do you feel more open and free or more constricted? If the former, well done; if the latter, be okay with that. Don't judge your present-moment inability to be compassionate! Do some journaling or meditate or pray or embrace whatever you're feeling. It's not wrong. And it's temporary. With work, you can begin to have compassion for others and how they are, who they are, and what they're doing or not doing. Your inner peace is on the line here. It is directly related to your physical health. It's worth the effort.

Conflict

Many of us feared—and thus avoided—conflict during our childhood. We learned the hard way that we shouldn't challenge our parents or rock the boats of people who we perceived as belligerent or trying to control us. But for those on the path of growth and expansion, constructive conflict is welcome.

For example, if I yell at someone, "Put away your damn dishes!" it probably won't be received well. Though instructive, the energy isn't constructive. Angry expressions like this typically mean that there is an unmet need beneath the words. While it's okay to express some anger in a healthy way, the energy associated with this request doesn't set the stage for healthy conflict resolution.

Being able to access the underlying energies associated with a request will lead to a better outcome. Some communication styles have a recommended outline; for example, state your feelings first, then the specific action that brought those feelings up, and then verbalize the request and how you'll feel different if that request is honored: "I feel sad when you leave the dishes out. So please put them away, so I don't feel sad." While logical and often effective, to me there's an element of disempowerment at play. I'm giving some of my power away by stating that what that person does or doesn't do is responsible for my feelings. The words or actions of others may trigger me, but those wounds were already there ripe for the poking.

To put any form of blame or responsibility on the other person isn't fair to them. By owning our responses, we can instead say, "I feel sad when you leave the dishes out. I'm not asking you to do anything differently. I'm just stating how I'm feeling." No blame. No request. Just a statement of fact. I could even add, "I'm aware that your (in)action is bringing to the surface some unresolved wounding of the past, and for that I thank you." How do you think that may be received? A little better than "Put away your damn dishes!" yes?

With presence and self-awareness, I've just managed to state what's true without blame. In my experience, this type of request is often received by the other person as an opportunity to do something nice for you. No one likes to be told what to do, but in this way, the recipient may follow your nudge without resentment.

Feeling into the situation, the superpower of many empaths, can clue us in to what's really going on beneath the surface of what's being said to us. If I do something that triggers emotional upset in my partner, I can better respond to that by apologizing if necessary, and also empathizing. Something as simple as

"I understand what you're feeling" (if true) can be incredibly disarming to someone who's expressing their displeasure.

This doesn't mean that you should be a doormat, either; instead, it means to go through—not around—our emotional reactions and take complete ownership of our words and actions. It means consistently questioning our own motivations, and understanding those of others. With practice, eventually this can become the new norm. When someone says something that triggers me, I can either honor that someone feels they can speak their truth or get angry at them for speaking up. I assure you, the former is much more satisfying for all.

Imagine saying, "Thank you for expressing what's true for you. Even if I feel hurt, I can and do appreciate that you feel safe enough with me to share your concerns and feelings. Whatever you're feeling is welcome here. I embrace all of you." How do you think that might be received? We can respect others wherever they are and for whatever they say by being present enough to know that most of the time, what's being said isn't a personal attack on us; rather, it's a reaction to something unhealed in the other person. Knowing this, why would I want to catalyze more anger, hurt, or even shame? Sure, it's not fun to get yelled at, but what if we truly know that what others are saying isn't all that's going on? We can use our superpowers for good and let them inform us of what's really true under the words, and then respond appropriately rather than being triggered and reacting out of fear.

You already know that a quality conversation between differing viewpoints can lead to a better mutual understanding. As we learn to embrace conflict as both an inevitable part of our experience and an invitation to understand and thus connect deeper with another person, we can use the above skills for the betterment of all.

Creativity

To quote Jonathan Larson, "The opposite of war isn't peace. It's creation!" Creativity can be expressed through cooking, painting, personal style, drawing, home decor, sex, poetry, exercise, and so much more. From a healing perspective, any creative flow is better than no flow and the end result's quality or quantity is irrelevant.

When we get our creativity flowing, we receive more inspired energy from Source. Inspiration can be specific to an art form, catalyzing internal or external peace or curing a disease. Any creative movement or endeavor is better than stagnation. Get up. Move your body. Movement begets more movement and welcomes inspiration.

D'pression

Sadness is normal. Grieving is healthy. But we're taught that grieving is unattractive or worse, and we stop the grieving process by stuffing those feelings down and out of conscious awareness.

Most of us have a lot of sadness to manage. From the initial separation from Source till now, it all adds up. Pushing down all that sadness is like pushing a beach ball under water. You can only hold it down for so long before the pressure becomes too great and you're too tired to continue. Eventually, your grip on the beach ball weakens and it smacks you right in the face. That smack is what I call "d'pression." Among many factors, "d'pression" is not always or solely caused by having too much sadness; rather, it's quite often the end result of not processing whatever sadness we've had.

If we go to a medical doctor for d'pression we may receive a prescription for medication to balance the chemical depletion (which can be a symptom, not a cause), and it just might work! But no matter how much better you feel with the medication, the repressed emotions of months or decades of sadness can be eating away at you from the inside out because repressed emotions cannot be healed with a pill. If you need proof of that, ask anyone who stopped their meds without doing quality therapy first. They likely fell right back to where they were before the medication regimen began. This isn't bad or wrong.

The obvious observation is that antidepressants can provide temporary relief from d'pression by blocking access to the underlying cause. If your doctor and/or you believe you need your medication, please follow their instructions; I merely invite you to recognize what medications can and can't do, and to act accordingly. If we take ownership of what has happened and pursue the most holistically helpful therapies—in addition to medications as needed—we can shift our inner environment. Because it's up to us, I prefer to call this "me-pression."

After living in my new city of Portland for a while, I started feeling extra sad. It was understandable given that I'd just moved from the East coast, leaving everyone and everything I'd ever known behind, and had yet to connect with the locals. But I was too close to it to see what was happening. Eventually, the sadness grew strong enough to grab my attention in a different light. I knew I had to change something or it would get worse. Knowing that fighting creates more of what I was trying to fight, I instead sat with my sadness.

You know that phrase, "Feel it to heal it"? I felt it, but nothing healed. I later intuited that "Feel it to heal it" is incomplete. I had to take another step. I had to love it. Feel it. Love it. Heal it.

"Love me-pression? How can anyone love something that feels so horrible?"

It's not easy to love one's sadness, and it's a lot harder to do so when we've been taught to judge it so harshly. But I've learned not to judge what's natural. And grief, as the body's way of healing loss, is as natural as waking up in the morning. What's natural shouldn't be fought. What's natural should always be embraced and even revered. When we can truly embrace whatever exists, the judgment fades. What we no longer judge loses its energy. Its charge is reduced. With enough practice, sadness can potentially pass through us. I healed myself without any pills.

One of the more common aspects of me-pression is a feeling of aloneness. We don't feel like we belong. No one gets us. Only other HSPs understand us, but we lack the enthusiasm to meet them. If we do get out, we tend to be the outlier in most gatherings. So we isolate.

More alone time typically leads to more feelings of separation and more sadness. Intense and prolonged sadness is, among other factors, an end result of a lack of connection. That's not what we're here for. If it's just occasional, isolation is probably not a big deal, but if solitude becomes our default social setting, we're not serving ourselves or others. Please know that there are millions and millions of fellow empaths and HSPs we can connect with. Whether online or by starting or joining a local Meetup group, there are always opportunities to connect.

We're all born sensitive and feeling connected. But events and circumstances during and even pre-birth can affect our health. It is widely known that if a pregnant woman smokes, so does her baby. I deduce an extension of that: if Mom is d'pressed, the depleted brain chemicals that can lead to that diagnosis may also be lacking in her baby, potentially creating a sense of having been born grieving. This isn't meant to blame you for your child's woes or permission to blame your mom for your challenges—blame never helped anyone. Rather, this is a reminder that during pregnancy we are sensitive to not just the physical health but also the emotional health of our mother.

Empaths and HSPs have the additional challenge of managing the sadness of others. That grief can be from our own parent or family lineage, or that of friends, partners, employers, or even that of animals or the planet. The empath's main tool, albeit an unconscious one devised by the child's mind for survival, is absorbing others' grief in order to resonate with and connect to the person we're holding it for.

This cumulative and continual absorption of other people's sadness is insidious and explains why you can feel it and feel it and feel it in an attempt to heal, but no matter how much you do, it's still left unhealed. What's happening is that you are releasing other people's grief and because prior to this book you've not yet been trained on the more effective preventative techniques, the energy is reabsorbed—sometimes within days or even hours. This continual re-manifestation of empathic sadness is what I've called, riding the hamster wheel of healing. We work and work and work and get nowhere.

Having absorbed the grief of others long enough, we become a grief magnet of sorts. Other people pick up on that vibration and dump their problems on us. And because we don't know otherwise, we listen and take it on. And on, and on. . .

The process of empathic sadness is often as follows: We feel the grief of our caretakers and family and try to help, but we can't heal them no matter how much we absorb because it's not our job to do so. As we age we find other people—or they find us—whose grief we absorb. These encounters and relationships allow us to continue the pattern of trying to heal others—but these too are never effective. And when that doesn't work, we look to an even bigger stage and may go into the healing arts, traditional or alternative or both, in an attempt to heal others or even the planet and find ourselves saying, "I feel like I've got the weight of the world on my shoulders."

But carrying the intense sadness of individuals, families, communities, nations, or the world was and never is our job. Whether you're a healing practitioner seeing three or 30 people a week or a good friend who is always feeling drained being there for others, you still might not feel like you're making enough of a dent because you're trying to fill an inner void that can't be filled with anything external to ourselves.

Empathically absorbed sadness has to be returned to the original source. The Body Scan / Return to Sender exercise in Chapters 4 and 5 has brought peace and ease to many of my clients. These tools teach you how to give back the energy that has never been yours to carry. The recipient can then do with it what they need to. While that process can seem uncaring at first, eventually you begin to see that doing so is best for all involved parties. Giving back what others came here for is an amazing form of self-care and perhaps the ultimate form of caring for others, too. To hold onto anything like that for them is arrogant if you really think about it. How can you, your own small self, be responsible for your parent's sadness, your lineage, or even that of the collective? It's a belief that is a mirage—a powerful one but untrue. And just like a mirage, the closer you get to it, the more aware you become that what you're seeing is a figment of the mind.

Diet

Tom and Mary are finishing up their dinner at home and Tom takes dessert out of the oven. Mary, slightly disappointed, asks Tom, "How come you always cut the ends off the apple pie? That's my favorite part!"

Tom replies, "Funny. I don't know. I always have done that. Come to think of it, my mother did that as well. I'll call her right now and find out why."

Tom calls his mom and asks, "Mom, how come you always cut the ends off the apple pie?"

His mom laughs and says, "I don't know. I always have done that. You know, I think my mother did that as well. Why don't you call Grandma and ask her?"

Tom then calls his grandmother. After the cordial greetings, he asks, "Grandma, how come you always cut the ends off the apple pie?"

Grandma laughs out loud and says, "Because when I was learning to bake we only had a very small pan!"

And so, the apple (pie) doesn't fall far from the tree. While our parents had the best of intentions for us, we should remember that, typically, they were following the ideas their parents taught them many years ago. Our parents may have made some changes as they became adults, but quite often the patterns of what's right and wrong and what is healthy and unhealthy (and how to make a pie!) are ingrained in them from their childhood. Among these hand-me-down belief systems is, of course, diet.

Times change, and so does our understanding of heath, science, pain, and illness. While some people repeat the dietary patterns of their childhood, many of us have experimented to find what works best for each of us. Sadly, when it comes to diet, the conclusions of experts seem to change as often as each year's styles of shoes. Everyone has a theory, and all swear they're correct. And with corporate lobbying and the possibility of biased research, how can you know for sure what's best for you and not fall prey to disingenuous advertising and subjective marketing? What's an Empath to do?

The Empath Diet, obviously!

I once ordered Chinese takeout at one of those places where the kitchen is right behind the cashier. You can see the cooks, and they can see you. Shortly after I ordered, I witnessed the two cooks arguing with each other. When I shared this with my friend, who is Chinese, she said, "That's just the way we talk to each other— loudly!" But I could feel that there was animosity between the two cooks, and when I got home, my first bite felt horrible. The food felt lifeless, lacking taste. This was my first realization that everything we ingest contains the energy of those who prepared it.

The Empath Diet emphasizes awareness of each food's inherent energetic state and also how it is grown, distributed, prepared, and served. If it's made by an angry cook, you're eating the energy of anger. If you prepare your meals quickly and when stressed, you're eating the energy of anxiet-me and the reaction to that, often called "fight or flight." If your food has been processed by machines programmed by people who are only in it for the profit (junk food), you're eating the energy of greed in addition to the physically harmful preservatives, colorings, and flavor and texture enhancements. If what you're eating has pesticides, you're eating the energy of death. And if you're eating muscles or byproducts of a factory farmed animal, physically, you're eating remnants of growth hormones, antibiotics, and so on, and metaphysically you're eating the energy of torture and the toxicity of the animal's fear prior to and during slaughter—or even their entire lifetime's pain and suffering.

Conversely, if you're eating organic vegetables and fruits, you're absorbing the groundedness of the root vegetables, the spirit of the plants, and the energy of the organic farmer who probably cares about his produce a lot more than mass-produced profit-centric farming practices.

Empaths and HSPs need to think of everything as energy, including food. And we'll likely feel better and be more vibrant eating higher vibration organic foods, low to no gluten, much less or no refined sugars, and more raw or warmed as opposed to cooked whenever possible. That's not solely because I think so, or because millions of others do, but because ingesting higher vibration foods that are prepared lovingly makes sense energetically.

Some of you, for a variety of reasons, may have tried eating healthier and felt worse initially. Certainly your individual constitution has an effect, as does your culture, heredity, and environment. But if you have initially felt worse changing to a cleaner diet, try opening to the possibility that you may be detoxing energetic or physical remnants of years or even decades of lower-vibration foods. Also do an honest internal inquiry: What is my neuro-association with this food? Ask yourself if eating what's known to be healthy for most people can have the effect it's having on you, in and of itself.

In addition, your energy when preparing your meals affects both the food and your ability to absorb the nutrients. Part of the reason people used to regularly say grace at the beginning of the meal was to cultivate a state of gratitude in their body before eating. This boosts the body's ability to absorb the nutrients.

What about carbs-fats-proteins? Which should we focus on and which should we minimize?

Logically, if someone is lifting weights, they should be more conscious of protein input. And for those looking to lose weight, they should certainly be aware of excessive carbohydrate consumption in addition to the possibility of emotional eating. But I'd like to discuss another matter, or non-matter, as it were.

The energy within each food or drink is as (or for some, more) important than its physical makeup.

What will vibrate higher: a raw organic carrot or a "pastry" made with processed sugar and chemicals? The answer is obvious, but making and acting upon the better choice can be difficult at first. I like to say, "*I get* to eat fresh fruits and vegetables" rather than think that my choices are limited. No one wants to feel limited. I also don't want to let my tongue and its learned fondness for animal fat and sweets rule my mind. In fact, after a short time avoiding animal products and sweets, I've developed an aversion to them, the anti-sweet tooth. It comes down to making wise choices in line with what your body, not your mind thinks you need.

I prefer *eating to live* rather than *living to eat*. No worries if you're the latter, but I will ask you, "Are you craving sweets because you're missing the sweetness of life? Are you eating what's familiar while potentially denying or ignoring how doing so negatively affects you? Are you living your life's purpose and managing your emotions well enough that you don't need to overindulge in food to make up for the feelings of emptiness or despair?"

I'm just asking questions.

For so many of us, food was the original control mechanism used by our caretakers. We were promised dessert if we ate our main course, or we were rewarded for good grades with fast food. How many of us to this day reward ourselves or our loved ones for major accomplishments with a special meal and/or a drink? "I'll drink to that!" we say. And how many of us try to soothe another person's emotional pain with food or a drink?

"Can we all just be quiet; I'm trying to concentrate on my food!" she said to us. I don't think I was alone in my initial reaction of shock to this request at my friend's birthday gathering at one of NYC's premier restaurants. But in retrospect, I get it. She just wanted to enjoy her meal. Is that so wrong? But so many of us have inherited the constructs of being social while eating. At her request, we all got quiet and slowed down. We thus began to taste the intricacies of the many flavors. Wow, what a difference!

Distractions while eating, whether they're social or reading or watching TV, can affect your brain's ability to know when you're full, leading to poor digestion and/or overeating. I've heard that the satiation response lags 15 minutes behind your body's awareness that you're full. That means that when your brain gets the message saying that you're full, you've already overeaten 15 minutes' worth of food. This can be minimized if we're more present with our food. Give yourself the gift of your meal's flavors and textures by chewing appropriately, knowing that digestion begins in the mouth. Inhaling your food doesn't allow you to taste what's there nor does it allow for effective digestion.

Whenever possible, eat higher vibration foods. Eat them slowly, and choose your company wisely. You will notice a difference.

Digestion

Digestion challenges are typically end results of either not eating the proper balance of nutrients, or if we are eating well, not absorbing those nutrients well. So the question then becomes, If I'm eating well, why aren't I absorbing the nutrients? And the answers can be varied.

Gest comes from Latin, meaning "carry; bear." Most of the people I work with have been carrying energies of others for a long time. You could say they've digested them. Because this is something we do as opposed to something that is done to us, I prefer to call digestive disorders, *my-gestion* challenges.

My-gestion challenges are from energetic blocks that don't allow our bodies to absorb the nutrients from our food. If we're carrying the energies of others, it's only logical that our my-gestive system will be overburdened. We need to access our own body's information highways by going within and letting ourselves become informed of what is there.

Oftentimes we'll see grief in the organs of my-gestion and elimination, but that's not always the case. While the more generalized maps, charts, and diagrams that have been out for so long can and often do tell a truth, it's important to remember that those maps of illness and the underlying causes won't always be correct.

We should address each ailment as an opportunity to discover something new using our beginner's mind. Like an experiment in which we don't know the outcome, we should open to whatever needs to emerge. Sometimes inner readings will guide us on a long, circuitous journey to get to the truth. While that may be frustrating, why fight it? It's for a reason, even if we don't know the reason in the moment. Eventually, all becomes clear.

The tools in Chapters 4, 5, and 6 will teach you how to explore and heal my-gestive challenges.

Drugs

Pharmaceuticals have their place. Who hasn't taken an antibiotic to cure an infection? But Empaths and Highly Sensitive Persons (HSPs) need to be extra careful about using over- or under-the-counter pharmaceuticals. Because we feel everything, our side effects can be a lot worse than the side effects for others. We can feel the energy of the drug designer, the company's marketing team, their advertisers, the distribution network, the pharmacist, the cashier, and so on, in addition to feeling the well-documented, physical side effects.

If the instructions on your bottle of aspirin indicate that you need X milligrams, empaths and HSPs can probably get the desired effect with half or even one-third of that. I have had many clients who have said they get sick and burdened with side effects from even typically benign pharmaceuticals. I ask them to inform their doctor that they are easily and negatively affected by medications and to ask their doctor if there is a less threatening drug that can be recommended—or at least get an approval for using a lesser dosage. We have to communicate our needs to our medical providers!

Another option is to become more aware that our physical body responds to every thought we have. Thinking, "I wish I didn't have to take this damn medication" while you are ingesting it can create a negative internal environment, potentially affecting you in negative ways. How do you think your body will respond to speaking and feeling love and appreciation instead? Try thinking, "While I may not like taking this medication, I can love it and be appreciative that it exists and can help me on this day." Do you think your internal environment might respond better to these types of thoughts? Please don't test this on known allergens! Start out small, and work *with* your body, not in defiance of it.

I am a big fan of homeopathic remedies when indicated. I've yet to hear of a negative side effect, and despite the establishment's desire to question and debunk homeopathy, homeopathic remedies can be very helpful for many people, even more so when formulated by a naturopathic doctor or homeopath who can tailor the remedy to your specific needs.

Let's be open to the benefits of all forms of medicine without needing to tear down a modality to make ourselves look or feel superior. Judgment can hinder the healing process, and anger toward a typically (or hopefully) well-intentioned practitioner doesn't serve you or your healing.

I remember looking around a pharmacy and noticing that almost everything I saw was designed to bury discomfort or pain. Runny nose? Take a decongestant. Cough? Take a cough suppressant. Diarrhea? Take a. . . well, you get the picture. It's deeply embedded in our culture that any physical and even emotional discomfort has to be relieved immediately and singularly. But at what cost?

In the above examples, a runny nose can be grief trying to exit the body. A cough can be from a lung irritant that we've taken in. And diarrhea can be the body's natural detoxification of food poisoning or the releasing of accumulated emotional or physical toxicity. Granted, these aren't fun and can feel horrible in the moment, but intentionally clogging up the very pathways that are designed to help us heal us can't be a good thing in the long run.

As far as non-pharmaceutical drugs, or recreational ones, if you choose this path please use them consciously. Be aware that you may be potentially bypassing doing your inner work in favor of feeling good artificially. Bypassing will always catch up with you.

Ego

When in the presence of someone deemed an enemy, our typical responses are to fight back or flee. If survival is at stake, we'd do whatever it takes to be the victor. But what if we acted as if we're our own enemy? Would we do whatever it takes to fight back against ourselves? Ridiculous, right? Or is it? How many of us have beaten ourselves up for not being good enough, smart enough, pretty enough, wealthy enough, or even spiritual enough? And did you then beat yourself up for beating yourself up?

The ego, that part of us that is designed to keep us safe, is also designed to challenge us. For even as we look outside the self for perceived enemies, to paraphrase Pogo, eventually we realize that enemy is within.

Too many of us try to defeat our own ego as if it is the enemy, but is that really working? Clearly, that isn't the best strategy. What if we treated our ego as if it were our friendly opponent rather than an enemy? It's time to send it a Friend Request!

An opponent is someone we play a game against. Ideally, we enjoy each step, strategy, or process and even if we lose, we still had fun. Think about playing against someone in chess, or being part of a doubles match in tennis, or being part of a team playing against another team as is the case in baseball or any sport where there is both a defense and offense. (Personal peeve time: golf, bowling, skiing, and the like are not sports. You're only playing against yourself. Without defense, you're only doing the best you can, and if someone has a better score they win. Despite appearances, it's a solo competition. I thank you for indulging me.)

If you lose against an opponent in tennis, it's not a big deal, right? You likely enjoyed the process enough to do it again. In each case, your opponent isn't your enemy; just someone or a group of people you have to play a little bit better than to claim victory. Can you imagine how your life experience would differ if you thought of your ego as an opponent and not your enemy?

Because the ego is a linear-based entity and is really good at what it does, we can't use logic or linear thinking against it and expect to win. That would be like trying to outwit a computer. Computers don't reason. To live a quality life, we need to understand this truth and deal with the ego as if we're opponents playing a game using the tools with which there can be success. If we can use tactics that the opponent doesn't understand, we can have a better experience and even win a few rounds!

First tactic? Awareness.

I can't speak for people across the planet, but everyone I've ever worked with has thought negatively about themselves. It would seem to be the norm, not the exception. We tend to marvel at those who seem to have it all together, but do they? How many famous people are still striving for something and end up hooked on attention or drugs? How many millionaires won't rest easy until they're billionaires? How many already attractive people get plastic surgery or paint their face with toxic chemicals to hide a perceived flaw? How many of us compare ourselves against these seemingly idealized persons and fail to match up? When someone's reality and their appearance are not aligned, I call this phenomenon FaceBookFace. When we present ourselves as more successful, better looking, wealthier, or just having more fun than others, that's FaceBookFace. It's a sham(e)! Be aware that very few people truly have it all together. We've been judging ourselves against a benchmark that barely exists!

Second tactic? Acceptance.

We weren't born thinking we're bad or wrong. Somebody had to convince us of that. We need to accept that we've been lied to. And we need to accept ourselves as perfectly imperfect bipeds just trying our best to heal our wounds. Accept the full range of being human.

Third tactic? Don't fight your ego as if it's the enemy.

What we fight gets more energy. What we befriend, softens. What we resist or despise gets more energy. What we love, dissipates. And if we love unconditionally, anything unlike love is transformed into love. Your ego only wants to play a game. It distracts you from doing your inner work because it fears it will no longer exist if you become privy to its ways—game over. When we judge the self or others, the ego wins. Instead, notice that thought and the potential reaction of self-criticism and then choose self-love: "That's my ego yacking away. I see you. Thanks for your recommendation, but I'm choosing love right now. I love you and thank you for keeping me on my toes."

Wouldn't that be a more peaceful existence? With practice, you can notice when your ego or your heart are in control. With more heart-centered presence practice, you can turn down the volume on the ego. It'll never go away, and that's a good thing. So why not work with it and even enjoy the process, just as you would a game of chess?

Enlightenment

To many of the spiritual seekers I've met, enlightenment is the grand prize awaiting them at the end of all the work they've been doing. For many people, it's the end goal that needs to be attained for any chance of healing or happiness, or for sharing themselves with the world. When I hear these reasons for seeking enlightenment from my clients, I like to challenge these assumptions. I share with them:

1. There is no guarantee that even after enlightenment there will be no pain.
2. To paraphrase a teacher I once worked with: If you're a Type A go-getter and you attain enlightenment, congratulations, you're now an enlightened Type A go-getter.
3. Seeking enlightenment is actually closing down the pathway whereby enlightenment might occur.

Seeking anything spiritual is like a dog chasing his own tail. He'll spin and spin and because he's excited, the tail wagging makes catching the tail even more challenging. But as soon as he slows down, his tail will relax making it easier to catch. The spiritual path toward enlightenment isn't much different.

Seeking a future condition takes you out of the moment. And present moment awareness is what gives us the opportunity to make decisions based on truth rather than a pattern. Doing inner work can help reduce the old pattern's pull on you. To me, the best way of understanding growth is being able to recognize an old pattern and consciously deciding not to follow it. When we do this, we make better choices in the moment and create a better future.

With presence, we can act as an enlightened soul might— by accessing enlightened thought patterns, slowing down, and listening to intuition long before enlightenment is actually attained. No more seeking. No more self-criticism. Less worry.

I asked the leader of a spiritual eco-village in Costa Rica who many thought to be enlightened (he never used that word) if he is worry-free. He thought about it for a bit, then leaned over and whispered in my ear, "I worry . . . (long pause) . . . less."

Entities

Though less common than many other concepts and challenges listed here, on occasion I do work with those who feel like they're carrying foreign entities. Typically, these clients have already tried many modalities that at best have given temporary results, the reason being that the underlying cause had yet to be identified and healed.

Sure, some practitioners with energetic awareness and healing skills can help you clear out an entity, but without finding out and working with why the entity is attracted to you, healing will only be temporary.

To use a visual, picture a hole in an aura. The hole is in the shape of a lock. The entity is the key that enters the lock and stays there. You can clear it out, ask it to leave, and so forth, but wouldn't it make more sense to change the lock? With detailed inner work, we can ask the body to show us what created the hole to begin with. And we should fill in that hole from the inside out. If the hole is an end result of fear, for example, what is that fear about? What is the message it is carrying? If we heal that fear, the entity will no longer want to be there. It will exit on its own and not return because there'd be no place conducive for it to live.

Exercise

Empaths and Highly Sensitive Persons (HSPs) typically do better participating in low-impact exercise as opposed to high-impact exercise. The forms of exercise that are typically most aligned with our needs include walking, gentle jogging, tai chi, qi gong, pilates, yoga, and so forth, as opposed to lifting heavy weights. This doesn't mean modest weightlifting can't be helpful; rather, it is a reminder that if a person's body is already filled with tension, lifting heavier weights than necessary can add to that tension.

As a former personal trainer, I can share a few helpful tips:

Change your mindset. Many people develop wrist problems, typically diagnosed as repetitive strain injury (RSI) or carpal tunnel syndrome. While the diagnosis may be accurate, consider that it may also not be. By that I mean that your state of mind when doing any action or exercise determines your energetic and emotional state and that in turn affects your physiology and resistance to pain and illness. If you're doing a day job you hate— for example, a desk job that includes lots of typing—typing will seem a bore at best. If you enjoy your day job that includes lots of desk work, then typing won't be perceived as a nuisance. How do you think these perceptions of what looks the same on the outside affect your inner world? Two similarly healthy persons doing similar activities can have very different internal experiences.

Clearly, the person hating his job is more likely to develop pain and stiffness than the person who is loving her job.

Incorporate full range of motion, whenever possible. Let's take that same joint as mentioned above: the wrist. Your wrist is an amazing apparatus that can flex, extend, and is involved in supination, pronation, and rotation, but too often when we do more Western exercise, we only do flexion and extension. Tai chi, for example, incorporates gentle rotations and can help prevent or minimize wrist pain.

Follow the rule of the Double E: Exhale upon Exertion. Take, for example, forward bend in yoga. If you can only forward-bend 90 degrees, breathe in, and when breathing out try to go just a tad farther. Repeat this process slowly. We have more physical mobility than most of us think but are limited by our muscle tightness, which is often the mind-body result of our own emotional rigidity or repetitive shorter-range movements. Just as the mind relaxes when we focus on the breath, our bodies also relax when breathing deeply. The mind perceives a sense of safety and allows us to relax more into the moment, and our muscles can then stretch beyond perceived limitations.

Fatigue

Fatigue, chronic or acute, is among the most common conditions for Empaths and Highly Sensitive Persons. But instead of wondering why this is, I think a more empowering question would be, *Given my extreme sensitivities and my (un)conscious desire to hold everyone's energy, how could I not be exhausted?*

Within this reframe is an acceptance of our own divine gifts. From a place of acceptance of what is, rather than fighting what is, we can work to attain greater clarity and healing. Part of that clarity comes from understanding that by being an emotional and energetic sponge for years, if not decades, we've taken on energies that lead to stagnation as if it is our own. One woman in Seattle told me that she had been diagnosed with Chronic Fatigue Syndrome (CFS) and during the last 10 years had had some days where it was so bad she couldn't get out of bed. She then told me that after practicing my techniques for only four days, about 90 percent of that was gone.

While most people won't have that dramatic of a turnaround, I think it's good to share her story so that you know that it's possible to heal. There are so many factors involved in healing that to have this quick of a shift, one has to be ready—I mean *really* ready to make a change. By "really ready" I mean beyond verbalizing readiness; their body has to be ready for change, too.

Sure, diet can be a causative factor of fatigue, as can the environment at work or at home. Pains, challenges, illnesses, and, of course, lifestyle can also affect energy and fatigue. But for HSPs and empaths who have already made great strides in the aforementioned, it's typically over-empathy—high absorption of energy from others—that is the main culprit.

Misunderstanding and/or misusing empathic skills leads to feeling and then keeping too much of what's not ours. This is quite draining, partly because over-absorption isn't in alignment with your Higher Self. Your fatigue is a message telling you that you should make better, more informed choices in alignment with who you really are. By practicing the preventative tips detailed here in *Empathipedia,* you can notice a difference in a very short period of time.

Do your best to identify what and who you are truly responsible for, and work from there. Just do a little bit at a time. Clearing or even healing too much too soon can worsen matters because too much energy movement over too short a period of time can be quite a jolt to the system. Work with a teammate to determine what you're holding, where and whose it is, and take the appropriate steps as described in the Healing sections of this book.

Fear

How many of you have heard, "Feel the fear, and do it anyway"? That works well for Type A personalities, but for HSPs and empaths, "Feel the fear, and do it anyway" is an invitation to more overwhelm. Yes, it is true that we should feel whatever is real in any moment, and if fear is present, it is real—despite the sometimes-true acronym, False Evidence Appearing Real. While your fear may be based on something seemingly unreal to others, for you it can be as real as being an empath.

The newer paradigm embraces all aspects of self, whether they're real or not to others in the 3D world. When clients share things that might increase isolation (or worse) in the 3D world, I embrace their reality with the understanding that making them wrong doesn't help. Who am I to know what's real for another person? I've also found that the more uncommon their beliefs tend to be, the more pain they're in and the more they are trying to manage that pain. So I assume what's being presented is real for each person and at the same time feel into the underlying causes of the fear or belief. By addressing those aspects, I can guide people past their mind-created reality and into the body, where the truth rests dormant until excavated.

I invite you to embrace your fears, especially considering that they're often safety mechanisms. For example, if a bus is coming at you, the natural reaction of fear will motivate you to get out of the way. But judging your fears as wrong holds them in place and can actually add more energy to them. Accepting your fears can reduce their pull and allow you to feel into deeper parts of your true self for information on what these fears are about.

For example, Betty has a fear that Barney will leave her—even though he's shown no signs nor verbalized any thoughts of leaving. Her friends might say, "He's a good man, and you're a good catch. He wouldn't do that to you." But by accepting the possibility that he may leave, a deeper truth will emerge; for example, having been—or even felt—abandoned, typically by her former partner or her parent(s). If we process any of Betty's repressed emotions about those relationships, her fear will likely be minimized, sometimes dramatically, or at least enough to stay present to Barney's devotion to her.

Sometimes a reframing of fear can be helpful. For example, my very first expo lecture was in a room that held about 200 people, and only about five of those seats were taken. I was still so scared that just before I was about to speak, I approached my friend's booth, where he was doing Deep Emotional Release Bodywork. He had a way of tapping on a chakra while asking a question that somehow would bypass the mind. He asked me to lie down on his table and then asked me, "Are you scared?" and I surprisingly replied, "No." It was as if something other than me—or more precisely, other than my fear—was doing the talking. He then asked, "Are you excited?" and I said, "Yes," with equal surprise! He laughed and said, "Get off my table!"

That reframe helped me see that the symptoms of fear and excitement were often the same, only my perception of them differed. By knowing I was more excited than scared, I was better able to give the lecture without freaking out. I later heard a big-name professional actor talking about his nervousness before performing. He said that if those nerves weren't erupting before performing, he'd leave the art. He welcomed them fully as part of the process of getting ready to share his gift.

We all have various fears running large parts of our lives. For HSPs, the fear of not being liked, not caring enough, the fear of feeling too much, or saying the wrong thing as if we're walking on eggshells are among the most common. By acknowledging rather than judging those fears, they lose their strength. By befriending the shadow aspects, we can be more present to the truth and feel into any given situation and always know what to do or say. We can better remember that not everyone will like us, and that's okay. And by using the tools in this book, we can still feel the emotions of others, but only enough to consciously respond rather than unconsciously react.

It's important to become present to and heal our fears because the fearful mind limits accurate awareness and the ability to use our empathic skills. Overtaxed thought processes reduce our ability to determine whether what's arising is ours or absorbed from others. Intuition is negatively affected by too much fear. Fear mode catalyzes an always-searching mindset and a need to make sense of what lacks sense in that moment. Fear births and propagates conspiracy theories and seeks out other fearful minds to infect. Under duress, the mind can make an enemy out of a loved one, even people we've never met. (There is a wonderful *Star Trek Voyager* episode called "Nemesis" that illustrates propaganda's ability to make us see what isn't there.)

A fearful populace allows authoritarians who promise law and order to begin or continue movements for their personal aggrandizement. Fears left unchecked make our minds look for a strongman or something similar to save us, but that's looking outside ourselves to fix an internal misalignment, which will never work. Fear of the future manifests in longing for a past where we thought everything was wonderful, but that goes against our evolutionary impulse to grow and to adapt to new challenges and situations. Fear limits inward reflection and will point out (or make up) flaws in others to focus on. We have to heal ourselves so we don't get caught in the tidal wave of unloving words and actions. It takes a continuous conscious re-choosing to get into a place of love to better follow our own internal guidance.

Fear left unchecked can and will affect not just our minds but also our bodies. Fear can make the body shake. At first, the shaking is barely perceptible, but over time it worsens and eventually is given a dire diagnosis. Fear negatively affects thoughts, imagination, creativity, and our ability to connect with something greater than ourselves. Stay alert to fear, and work with it before it becomes problematic!

Fibro-not-my-algia

In my experience, the "F word" alluded to here but not specifically named is the end result of absorbing too much frustration, resentment, and anger belonging to others. Combine this with our own general frustration, resentment, and anger—even our frustration, resentment, and anger from not getting any relief—and this can form a very difficult group of symptoms that typically can't be healed at the root level by Western medicine.

As we would do with any symptoms, in order to heal at a deep level, we have to intuit the underlying causes and also the hidden message within those symptoms. If you haven't felt seen or heard, for example, or have lots of frustration about your current place in the world, your body will react negatively to that. Accepting what's true can begin to heal these energies within you. It involves not only understanding that certain persons were unable or unwilling to hear you but also befriending your reactions to those events. Some people may say you have to forgive the other person's actions; I'd add that we should do so from a place of compassion and understanding that the offender's heart has likely been closed by their own wounding. From that clarity, it's easier to see that everyone is just doing the best they can with what they've been given.

Frustration, resentment, and anger are among the most detrimental of energies—not only because of their own inherent potential to cause harm but also because we tend to judge these aspects of ourselves as negative. So our resentment of frustration, or our frustration with resentment or our place in the world, can be as detrimental as the initial energy itself, if not more so.

Step back and then step in, loving the self and perhaps asking, "How could I have known any better, given my understandings of the world and my experience in it?"

By doing the Body Scan detailed in Chapter 4, you can determine what's not yours and begin the energetic healing of the underlying causes of Fibro-not-my-algia. Any energies that are not our own should be returned to the source, as described in Chapter 5.

I've had a few interactions on social media about Fibro-not-my-algia that have gone nowhere. I really thought I was being helpful posting a blog about Fibro-not-my-algia on a F-word Facebook page, and as much as most were really appreciative, one in particular, not so much. She accused me of spamming. My first reaction was that I was appalled by her statement! I got defensive, and in retrospect, it probably looked like I was begging for her to understand I meant no disrespect. But she'd already made up her mind. And why not? We all project our past onto our future. When I finally stepped back from my emotional reaction, it was much easier to see she could have been projecting her past onto her present. As I got more in touch with my compassion, I was able to see clearer that she didn't know me at all, and perhaps had already been promised healing by dozens of practitioners. She was taking out her frustrations on me. And these were legitimate frustrations. The reality is that all I did was post a blog and all she did was react. As much as I could feel for her, whatever she thought or said to me was nothing more than what she thought or said. Had I gotten to that place sooner, I'd have saved myself a lot of heartache and time.

Can I give you some unsolicited advice? No one likes unsolicited advice!

Have you tried to help others and got back nothing but resistance? When trying to help someone in resistance even more compassion is needed, along with not taking anything personally to avoid more conflict. For some, the fear of getting healthy outweighs the fear of having daily bouts with illness or pain. There can be a secondary benefit they are receiving. For some, the attention placed upon them from others due to their symptoms may be the only way of receiving love and attention. I know as a kid I often exaggerated minor discomforts so that I could stay home from school. The secondary benefit I'd receive was more focused attention from my mother. Oh, and I could stay home and watch cartoons!

I have had a few clients who have said that their more serious illness has given them incentive to grow, and some were concerned that if they improved, they might not have that desire to continue growing—until they got sick again! If you see that someone you know is receiving secondary benefits from their pain or illness, monitor the depth of your relationship and their ability to take in information that could get them angry with you. Some may not want to hear it, but we feel compelled to say something anyway. As an empath, this desire to heal others could be a way for you to feel better! Use these potential scenarios to do your own work on attachment and expectations. Even if you have a good relationship, make sure there is enough trust to go to this level of openness. If there isn't, it's better to express empathy and not offer suggestions, even if your suggestions have proven invaluable for others in similar situations.

Some people may be ready to heal but because of their own unresolved issues with you, aren't able to hear *your* suggestions. Use your intuition to know how to work with anyone, and trust what you hear. Sometimes, it's best to let others be who they need to be without any intervention from you.

Grief

If I made someone cry when I was a kid, I'd be considered a bad person. Now, people pay me for it! I used to do anything to stop someone from crying, now I encourage it. Why? Because crying is your body's natural method of healing grief.

Not much different than white blood cells protecting the body from infectious disease, grief is activated in response to any type of perceived loss. If you've lost your favorite relative, or you've changed jobs or place of residence, or even if you've lost your favorite pen, your grief system is engaged. By allowing that sadness to be there, we can actually heal the loss with the most natural, inexpensive, and effective process available—crying.

Unfortunately, from the get-go we've been taught that crying is a no-no. Can you recall any of your earliest cries being supported? Instead we hear things like, "Big boys don't cry" or "You're going to ruin your makeup" or any other form of "Suck it up, weakling!" This is a perversion and an insult to our innate selves. These statements have perpetually created and concretized the belief that crying is bad, that having emotions is wrong. Years of this fallacy have led to millions of people repressing their most natural aspects of healing.

To this day, many of us don't feel comfortable seeing those we love or even ourselves expressing grief. At a funeral, we hear everything from the rather benign, "There, there, it's going to be okay" to "You'll see them again" or "They're not really dead," if someone believes in an afterlife. While well intentioned, this is not supportive. What people really need at a funeral is safe space to feel their feelings, maybe some tissues, or a heart-centered hug. We need invitations to our sadness—not obstructions—to truly heal. And yes, it's uncomfortable, but that discomfort is made progressively worse by our learned beliefs about crying as well as the judgments of others (either verbalized or energetically projected). The less we critique this powerful healing tool, the easier and quicker the entire process of healing.

The repression of grief is responsible for or at least a part of almost every ailment I've worked with. As recognized by Traditional Chinese Medicine, repressed grief is at least partly responsible for disorders of the lungs and large intestine, skin, ears, eyes, and sinuses. The latter two are the most obvious to me, in that the tear ducts are proximal to the eyes and sinus cavity. How do I know that this cross-referencing is true? Because when I encourage my clients to befriend and directly heal their grief, symptoms in the above-named areas vanish.

Grief is of the heart; anger is of the mind. To truly heal, we need to understand that the mind will do anything to keep you from feeling and healing, including pushing you toward the more socially accepted place of anger. It takes a very determined human to stay aware of this and allow the grief response to do what it is designed to do. We need to work through any and all blocks to access and heal this powerful and misunderstood emotion.

How?

Ideally, we allow what's there to be there. We consciously invite whatever has been buried to rise to the level of awareness. We cradle our own emotions with love and acceptance, just like we would cradle a crying baby. A baby doesn't understand linear thought or words; they respond to emotions and energy. You'd never tell a newborn she was bad or wrong for crying or try to explain to her that crying is bad and expect her to calm down. They respond to unconditional love and acceptance, and our adult emotions require the same type of attention to heal and transform the sadness at the root level.

Graduation

A few years ago, I began writing a book called *The Elephant in the Crystal Shop*" about New Age metaphysical teachings and communities. I wrote about what I perceived as spiritual bypassing, misunderstandings of the law of attraction, and a general lack of embodiment of what was being taught.

I shared the first few chapters with several trusted friends. Many of them enjoyed the content, and all stated that the book was sorely needed. Other readers added that the tone was unbecoming of me. They said that my observations and suggestions might not be seen as invitations to something better, and that my words were filled with projection, frustration, even anger. Interestingly, they still felt I should go ahead with publication. In retrospect, perhaps because they'd witnessed and become equally frustrated with the same things, they concurred with the energy behind what was presented in the book and supported me speaking my—make that *our*—truth, even though in hindsight, it was highly judgmental.

At that time, I justified the judgments by thinking, *Isn't it important for me to call out some of the more detrimental aspects of New Age, no matter how it comes out?*

Um . . . no.

And that's why I never finished it or published it.

Many systems, beliefs, movements, and philosophies have their benefits and drawbacks. But I'd entered a "holier-than-thou" state and had focused too much on what I perceived as the drawbacks of New Age, essentially blinding myself and potential readers to any of the good things that come from it.

It felt good to get all of that out of my system and then be supported in potentially sharing it with a bigger audience. My ego ate it up like a guru behind closed doors eating all the things he proposed we shouldn't. (Was that judgmental, an observation, or just a joke?) Well, we could use some levity!

What I see now is how much that tome was ego-based. The now-clearer reality is that if I'd really outgrown New Age, I would have mastered one of the most basic tenets of New Age and many religious and spiritual philosophies: nonjudgment. Clearly, I hadn't.

I had to ask myself, *What part of me needs to call out these New Agers? The ones who I used to study with, grow with, and learn from?* Was *The Elephant in the Crystal Shop* necessary? Was it supportive? Did it help anyone besides others who were stuck in ego to get a false, temporary hit of superiority via trash talking? Was this the kind of energy I really wanted to put out there in this already highly pained world?

I'm not the only one who failed New Age 101! Because one of the basic tenets of New Age is nonjudgment, I hadn't graduated at all. And neither, from what I've observed, have any of the writers of what seems to be the latest trend, calling "BS" on the entire New Age movement.

In the past several years, I've seen countless articles claiming that everything in New Age is BS. And based on the content, it was obvious they'd been in that world enough to learn the jargon and that they had been exposed to many of the principles. But they clearly hadn't mastered, or even gotten close to mastering what I now perceive as the most important precepts of all: compassion, unconditional love, and nonjudgment. And those who commented on or shared these posts and blogs did so with the same type of anger, frustration, and judgment I exuded years ago. They too, it appeared, had not done their homework.

So I'm reading these scathing articles and asking myself, *What part of them needs to call out the New Age movement?* and *Why are they doing so with such venom?* By speaking it, the projections inherent in the questions made themselves known: I was witnessing myself judging those who are judging! I then took ownership and asked myself:

What part of me *needs to call out these bloggers? If I truly think I've graduated from any school, philosophy, or movement, does that mean that what I've learned from those is wrong or bad? Does judging my own past ever serve me or others? If I hadn't gotten better at non-judgment or healed the anger I was feeling, would anyone buy the book or seek my services? (Well, besides other angry people!)*

It didn't seem helpful to trash-talk those seeking growth from my own egoistic and highly distorted reality. The truth is, I like to think I've learned a lot of great things from the New Age movement, perhaps more than the other paths I've studied. I've learned so much from all of them! To judge myself as better than those who follow any other path isn't a sign of growth but rather emotional immaturity.

New Age and other philosophies deepened my understandings of the mind-body connection and so much more. I like to think that the intuitive healing work I currently do is an augmentation of that, a version of "standing on the shoulders of giants" that I'd never attain if I hadn't gotten something positive out of my prior studies.

My graduation, it seems, was more of a realization that every bit of my past is as important as any moment of now.

Grounding

Being a city boy I'm not quite there yet with Earthing, the grounding practice of walking barefoot on the earth that has helped many people ground, improve their mood, and so much more, but even squeezing my toes in my shoes helps me receive energy from below. Whether on earth or carpet, we can visualize a cord going from our feet to the earth's core, getting more in touch with our solidity. At the same time, I like to do an ascending grounding (I know that's an oxymoron, but we're stretching ourselves, remember?). I make my spine as vertical as possible, "standing tall in my dignity" as one of my clients calls it, and I imagine the top of my head is connecting to the heavens.

Another grounding exercise I do is called a Presence Activation, which I will discuss in the Body Scan section of this book. There are many grounding exercises available that can be found online or elsewhere. Try them and see what works best for you!

Helplessness

Most of those I've worked with (self included) share something that for many of us hurts us even more than physical pain—an occasional, yet dreadful sense of helplessness. Who among us hasn't felt so overwhelmed with our own predicaments that we've lost any hope for a better tomorrow? Who hasn't thought of giving up the "good fight"? Has any empath or HSP not felt overwhelmed by the tides of social injustice, animal abuse, humanitarian crises, mass shootings, war, or natural disasters? Sometimes, it seems like our individual environment or even the whole world has gone mad and there's nothing we can do about it.

But there is. There always is.

When anxious, stressed, and overwhelmed, the mind thinks, *If only I could figure out what I'm anxious about, then I could do something about it.* And as logical as that is, it's trying to escape the unpleasantness of the situation with linear thought. Linear thought doesn't acknowledge stress as a teacher; rather, it convinces us that stress is an enemy that needs to be defeated ASAP. The mind will eventually make a plan, and it'll seem like a good one. But that strategy won't be Source-inspired. At most, that approach will get you out of immediate turmoil—which isn't horrible—but longer lasting and more effective methods typically don't originate in the mind.

Feeling helpless is made even worse by the conditioning we receive as children that knowledge equals praise and lack of knowledge equals shame. Do you remember raising your hand in school to show everyone that you knew the answer? Did you crave hearing your teacher say, "You're right! Great job!" And of course, the converse is also true. We're shunned or made fun of if we don't know certain things. In fourth grade, I was sent to a special class because I couldn't say the sound, "th" well. I felt rejected, ashamed, and of course, dumb. Granted it's a small example (I did get picked on for other reasons, too), but the feeling is the same:

there was something wrong with me, and I was a loser. We were never taught the value of a mistake in school. Instead, we had to get it right or we'd get a big F on our report cards and risk not graduating to the next year's program—FAILURE.

But mistakes are how we learn. Sometimes, lessons aren't as relatively benign as an assignment at school. Sometimes we fail at relationships. We fail to make a good living. We fail to heal something or to remain healthy once we get there. We overspend or invest in something that goes belly-up. LOSER.

The ego identifies with certain aspects and makes those known to others. While playing a trivia game or just interjecting a random fact into a conversation, the ego is always looking for praise. It can filter out anything negative and dares anyone to tell the emperor he's naked. Haven't you met a lot more people who will say they're above average in intellect than those who say they're dumb? And of course, we've all heard the narcissist claiming to know more than certified experts at pretty much anything. The need to believe we are—or at least be seen as—intelligent mars our experience of seeing the world as a mystery, learning as fun, or reveling in the uncertainty.

When we are overwhelmed, the mind goes to the fear place: *I don't know what to do! I don't know what my next move should be. I can't deal with the stress, the turmoil, the unpleasantness of it all.* Oftentimes, self-criticism kicks in: *I'm useless. I'm stupid. I'm a loser. I* should *know how to manage, to heal, to intuit, to. . .* You get the idea.

We have to accept that there are some things we just can't know. Sometimes, we don't know something because we don't have access to that knowledge, or perhaps something is beyond our current level of understanding. But if we work through these fears of looking or even being unintelligent—and I do mean through, not around—we will always be informed of what to do, when, how, and with whom in response to any situation.

In my experience, Source is always there to provide an answer to any inquiry. All we have to do is tune in. But we can't tune in well when in emotional chaos or fear. It's not easy, but as soon as you catch yourself in overwhelm and/or trying to figure things out, observe that and set a goal to get quieter. Focus on the breath, or use the Presence Activators discussed in the Body Scan section of Chapter 4.

For example, when in financial disarray, Source might not give you the winning lottery numbers, but it will show you how to best use your gifts to earn money. When we're open to a new relationship, Source might lead you to an online dating website or to a function to meet someone. If we are in need of healing and calm enough to notice, the right book or practitioner will find us.

But these instructions are not always so direct.

When we accept that wherever or whoever we're guided to is in our best interests, and that the Universe is always saying YES to us, even if it appears otherwise, when we can truly know this, we can quiet the mind and trust we'll be guided to the next best step! The inherent humility in a healthy surrender to something greater (as opposed to an unhealthy giving up) is the doorway to fulfilling our soul's contract and experiencing what we came here to witness and feel.

No matter what the issue is, there is always something we can do to ease back from the path of fighting and suffering. The information we need is always available to us, but we must first embrace not knowing how to respond and then allow ourselves to be informed. In this way, we replace helplessness with tangible action steps!

Immune System

Our immune system is marvelous. What an amazing feat of engineering, or evolution . . . or both! Given the proper conditions, it can heal just about anything. But so much of what we think, say, and do breaks down the immune system rather than keeps it functioning well.

According to psychoneuroimmunology, the study of the interactions among behavioral, neural and endocrine, and immune systems in the body, our immune system is directly affected by our thoughts and feelings. Each thought we have creates a brain chemical, or neurotransmitter, that communicates with the body via the nervous system using electrical signaling between neurons. It operates in both directions, hence the mind-body connection.

With this in mind, some people propose that we only allow ourselves to have positive thoughts. The problem is that people who don't allow themselves any negative thoughts are among the unhealthiest people I've ever met. Why? Because it's impossible to have only happy thoughts. In fact, the pressure to do so invites more self-criticism because what's being asked isn't possible! So when it comes to what weakens or boosts our immune system, I propose that we omit labeling our thoughts as "good," "bad," "happy," or "negative" and replace those adjectives with the following: "exclusive thoughts" or "inclusive thoughts."

Exclusive thoughts are judgments about any parts of ourselves or others, or life en masse. Exclusive actions are fighting illness, other people, and even fighting life. When we focus on the differences between ourselves and others—many of whom we may never have met—this is exclusive thinking. Thoughts of repeated anger, rage, jealousy, violence, fear, and so on will weaken our immune system's ability to heal pathogens and illness.

Inclusive thoughts are those that do not reject any part of ourselves or aspects of life, or life *in toto*. Inclusive thoughts accept life on life's terms. We may not like certain things, but as long as we're here we have to acknowledge and accept what exists before trying to heal what we don't like. Opening to bigger-picture or soul-level awareness is one way to catalyze inclusive thinking. Working with life and its challenges, learning, sharing our gifts, being on a love-based mission, having a support network, being vulnerable, honest, authentic, open, and humble can strengthen the immune system.

We have to accept that we're going to have both exclusive and inclusive thoughts. As we accept all of ourselves, more inclusive thoughts and actions will naturally arise.

Joints

While it's common to blame aging for joint pain, not everyone who hits a certain age will experience joint pain. Meaning that while age certainly is a factor, aging is not the only cause of painful joints.

Our bodies are designed to age with grace, but by the time we're older, most of us have accumulated enough emotional and physical toxicity from resisting life on life's terms in addition to the constrictive thoughts, limited exercise, unhealthy foods, and genetic issues that make aging painful.

Spiritual and emotional flexibility allows us to question, challenge, and change beliefs and heal our fears. As we patiently become more accepting and heal resistance, unhealthy beliefs, fears, and the like, emotional flexibility follows. Emotional flexibility "lubricates" our joints. If you are experiencing joint pain, in addition to making changes in mindset, diet, exercise, and so on, go within to ascertain where you've been inflexible in your inner or outer world. Because the mind and body are intimately connected, stepping into a new way of being can lessen joint pain.

Knowledge

We are information-seeking machines. How many books have you read? How many have you bought and have yet to read? Do you, like most of us, have a stack of books at home waiting for your attention? How many online articles and pages do you have in your Reading List or have bookmarked for a later date?

Reading *Empathipedia* or any other book is good, but aren't you tired of just good? Don't you want great? Let's take an honest look at what self-help books can and cannot do or provide, and learn how we can maximize our own results.

Weapons of Mass Distraction: If you truly believe that any book's tips can be of help, you'll have to really work hard to stay on track. The mind is not your friend; it'll try to take you out of the game whenever possible. So try to witness your inner opponent (ego) doing what it does so well, and accept it. Why? Because fighting your inner opponent hasn't worked yet. Embrace your desire to check your email. Acknowledge your random thoughts about dinner or politics. And without beating yourself up for being human, accept that these are normal.

Energetic Transmission: One of my Buddhist teachers pointed out that while it's great to read a book, it's a lot better to be taught by a master, or at least someone who knows more about a subject than you do (mastery isn't necessary to teach others!). He said there is an energetic transmission from the teacher/author that can help us to assimilate the information deeper and faster than reading a book. I have found energetic support to be vital in learning and healing. When a teacher, author, or healer holds sacred space, the recipient receives the benefits of an energetic transmission. A good teacher lovingly challenges the recipient to go just beyond their comfort zone, which is where growth really happens. Of course, people who are super-sensitive can feel the energy of the author's written word. No matter what you're reading, be aware of the potential of energetic absorption from whoever wrote it—especially if you read online message boards!

Consistent Application: If you read a book that proposes to teach the basics of bike riding, would you be able to ride a bike right away? Do you think you could read a book on learning a new language and quickly become fluent? In the bicycle example, you have to get on the bike and practice until you get it. You may fall a few times, you may need someone to assist you, but either way you have to get on the bike and build up the muscle memory and create new neural pathways that make bike riding possible. In the case of learning a new language, you have to practice enough to become fluent. Very few can take a weekend immersion in Spanish and be totally fluent on Monday. How can we expect to read about the tools to become a skilled empath and expect to have it mastered right away without consistent application? Still, most humans think we can master the information just by reading about it.

Why do we do this? Because the steps seem so simple. The theories make so much sense, the mind will say, "Okay, I've got this. I can now go into a crowd or stressful situation and open my keyhole and I'll be fine." While that is possible, it's rather improbable, given that you've likely spent (insert your age here) years NOT doing those things! So, don't expect instant results. Do the work. Be patient. And if you don't want to do the work or be patient, ask yourself what trying to short-cut anything has truly gotten you. Then do the work.

Unrealistic Expectations: Books can be wonderful tools, but they're still just a tool. You have to use tools consistently and well to get any results. One of the biggest follies I've seen in self-help books is the well-intentioned but ultimately facetious belief that we can always heal what ails us on our own. Some can. I have countless testimonials from readers sharing the incredible but real results they've gotten using my tools. But some can't. Just do your best! And know that your best can vary day to day. (How much is your left brain hating me now?) If we knew everything in advance, there'd be no purpose in doing, trying, or learning anything. Release attachments to a specific outcome and all will unfold in perfect order!

Lone Wolf Syndrome: While reading can raise awareness, we can grow a lot faster by allowing others to be mirrors for our inner environment. I've had clients tell me they feel that they've mastered certain things I've shared with them, only to later tell me they were triggered by the same thing once again. Meaning, it's easy to feel aware or even super-conscious when you're alone or with like-minded people, but can you maintain the needed presence to not get triggered when you're with others who may not be on your path? While I understand how isolation can feel safer and therefore preferred, the world needs you to step up and share your gifts. You need to share your gifts to feel connected and vibrant.

To combat Lone Wolf Syndrome, team up with others you trust. I get that you may not be excited by the idea of working with others. Fears of exposure and being criticized often override the deeper truth—that vulnerability and authenticity are the keys to opening the heart, better connections, and the doorway to the body's intelligence. Wondering who to trust and how to find the right person is seen by some as a potentially circuitous and lengthy path when we'd rather just get it over with as soon as possible. Our desire for the quick fix has been worsened by the recent self-care paradigm that echoes medicines giving us the illusion we can control symptoms at our own whim.

Out of the perhaps hundreds of books I've read on self-care, none have mentioned that deeper healing is so much easier with a teammate than reading and subsequent self-work. Let's stop doing what we think is working but actually isn't (I can assume this to be true because, with all due respect, you're reading this book searching for answers) and challenge ourselves in a healthy, logical, and ultimately do-able way. Let's get past our own misunderstandings of how deeper layers are accessed and healed!

Law of Attraction

Do you remember when you first heard of the Law of Attraction (LoA)? Did it excite you? Wasn't it amazing to hear from people we trusted and admired that we can manifest the perfect job and partner, vibrant health, and financial abundance solely with mental focus?

Do you also remember when you got frustrated with the LoA? Did it sadden you? Did you ever ask, "Where's my _____? (fill in the blank); I've been focusing on _____ (fill in the blank with the same answer or add others) so intently, how come this isn't working?"

What you focus on expands, but the way the LoA was initially presented—or perhaps more accurately, the way so many of us received it—was that mental focus alone was enough to manifest what we wanted. However, the initial teachings lacked many key ingredients. One of which is alignment.

Example: Let's say you've been making $75,000/year for several years and you attend a wealth seminar. The leaders tell you that you can manifest ten times more, $750,000/year and you begin the process of making vision boards, sharing your dreams with others, and so forth. But after several months, nothing has shifted. What do you think has happened? Or not happened, as it were?

One possibility is internal misalignment, meaning your body doesn't believe what you're telling it. Each time you think about making $750K/year, your body is saying, *Yeah, right. Don't you see we've become accustomed to only making $75K/year? Who are you kidding?* To induce alignment, try reducing the desired outcome to something more believable. For example, try manifesting a 10 percent increase and see how it feels internally. Once the body is on board, that's one more manifestation step conquered toward increased abundance!

Another option is that it's not in the cards for you. Or it's not (yet) meant to be.

What? But the workshop leader said that we can deal our own hand!

I'll bet they did! But what do they know of *your* soul's needs? What if your current state of evolution wouldn't be able to handle a rapid and radical increase in income? What if a part of your soul wants to teach you about the value of slowly earning money?

Manifesting the perfect partner isn't that much different. Meaning, that by dating people, you get to experience what it's like to share aspects of yourself with another person. You also get to see where your blocks to open-hearted connection may be. You get to learn, via an experience, what or who might work for you and what or who won't. If we found someone right away, we might not appreciate them as much as we would if we had dated others in the past. So if the LoA is bringing you people you don't vibe with, recognize that they're only reacting to the energy you are sending out. Consider these meetings as invitations to work on the self to attract someone more in alignment with your beliefs and desires.

The LoA took off because it was something that promised bypassing doing the deeper work! But we now know we can't avoid the internal and external work in manifesting abundance or the perfect partner or vibrant health. Our work is what we've come here to do. And if it were as easy as just thinking about it, we'd all be millionaires already, living with the perfect person and in perfect health.

And even if that were true, would we be content? Would we feel fulfilled? Source knows our needs better than we do. Can we reexamine our desires and realign them to what Source has in store for us? To me, the LoA is fun to play with, but not nearly as effective as surrendering our ideas of what we think we should be or have and following subtle directions on how and who to be, what to do, and when.

Media

Our current environment of ever-present media can be taxing to anyone, but especially for empaths and highly sensitive persons! As we scroll through our Facebook feed, we can take in energy from each person's picture and their comments—and the replies to the comments. Not all of these comments are supportive ones.

Social media has given everyone a voice and as wonderful as that can be, it can also bring out the worst in us. The safety of a computer keyboard in a café or at home has given more people more opportunities to project their internal pain farther than ever before. Those without the tools to heal their wounds now have an increased chance of affecting and infecting others and aren't afraid to spew their venom all over the Internet. Earth is already a scary place for many of us, only made worse by the proliferation of always available, often uncompassionate social and mass media.

Social media is also a way for mainstream media to share its message wider than ever before. By analyzing the headlines and click bait, we can get a sense of how mass media most often appeals to us: fear.

Mass media know that fear sells. And as corporate entities, their profits are often their only concern. Local news shows offer a constant barrage of negative occurrences in your own backyard. They're well aware that the more fear they instill, the more people will stay tuned hoping for some sense of security; however, fear begets more fear.

The more viewers stay tuned to network television, the more commercials they take in alongside the programming. The number of commercials for pharmaceuticals largely for fear-related illnesses that air during each newscast strikes me as interesting, sad, and highly manipulative.

More recently, slanted mass media political coverage, especially when immediately shared on social media, has added to the internal strife so many of us feel. Scarily, that is the goal of too many echo chambers. Politics, when done well, is the art of compromise. There is little to no chance that given our current state of evolution, most or all members of a given nation will think the exact same way. To truly thrive we need ideas from all sides. We need honest observation and conclusions of the past and present-day challenges to make rational decisions for the now and the future. And perhaps more importantly, the wisdom to know that lasting change happens incrementally external of the self just as it does internally. Mass media, however, plays upon our fears and ends up separating the masses into two or more conflicting parties. For empaths and HSPs, this is an assault on our senses and sensibilities and our understanding of the connectedness we are a part of.

The pain body of separation and fear decreases the ability to think logically, and attempts at reconciliation end up being a frustrating experience for all. Internet trolls inject their poison to make sure we all feel the pain they feel, and they're often quite successful. But as free-thinking, logical, and emotional beings that are becoming more and more awake, we have a say in how we respond to energetic and digital attacks. Without burying our heads in the sand, we can play their game or not. Although initially difficult, we can always choose the higher road.

The 24-hour rule has been my go-to for managing the intense emotions brought up by digital communications. I type my immediate reaction and then don't look at it or press send for 24 hours. Oftentimes, what was initially a long tirade of ego proving itself right, 24 hours later can be edited down to just a few sentences coming from a place of more understanding, and if I really do it well, acceptance and even love.

Today's world almost demands an immediate response to an email, comment, or article—we often like, dislike, comment, share, or reply immediately. While understandable, sharing our negativity is our lowest selves in action. If you can't wait 24-hours, I recommend taking several breaths before replying to an article or comment you find offensive and then making an honest internal inquiry: *Is my reaction factual or emotional? Is it true? Is it helpful? Is it necessary?*

Often, you'll see that the answers to the above are, respectively: emotional, no, no, and hell, no. At that point, it's easier to let others be who they need to be with no need to try to bring them to our side.

But what if what they're doing is wrong, or mean, or vindictive?

Does anyone really think that someone in their heightened emotional state of the pain body is going to read your comment and magically change their minds? As many teachers have pointed out, we should remember how difficult it is to change ourselves and how much more difficult or even impossible it is to change others.

I recall an online meme that read: "YES, I'LL CHANGE MY POLITICAL AFFILIATION BASED ON A FACEBOOK POST" SAID NO ONE EVER. You may feel that you know more than others. You may feel that you have a better way of being. You may shout that way of being from the rooftops or online, but until someone is fed up with their own closed-heartedness, they're not going to listen to other points of view and make a more heart-aligned decision. The ego wants to cling to its ways more than an empath wants to hang onto other people's emotions.

We can and should share our POV and be open to inviting others to a more heart-centered consciousness through our words and actions, while also allowing the needed time for others to play out their karma. Any judgments or attachments to others sharing our POV will typically lead to more internal misery. We can only be who we feel that we're meant to be and, hopefully, others will be inspired along the way. We need to remember bigger-picture and soul-level awareness is more conducive to healing than operating from the ego levels that prefer to blame others. Certainly, we should do our internal work and external work as well, but let that work come from the heart whenever possible; no one wins when it comes from a place of fear. Ever. From a place of love, everyone wins. Always.

Meditation

I often ask lecture or workshop attendees, "How many of you know that meditation is a good idea?" and typically about 90 percent will raise their hand. I then ask, "How many of you have a regular meditation practice?" and typically about 10 to 20 percent of those original 90 percent raise their hand.

Fascinating. We all know something is good for us, but few of us do it. The most common reason—underneath the common excuses—is that meditation is difficult. If we can't get good at something quickly, we often put it on the back shelf.

I think the concept, practice, and expectations of meditation are misunderstood. So many people try to achieve "quiet-mind," and while that may technically be possible, it's typically closer to impossible for most.

One of my meditation teachers asked her students, "What makes a good meditation?"

Being that she was a Buddhist, one student yelled out, "When you see the Buddha?" A Christian added, "When you see Jesus?" And another chimed in, "When you achieve 'no-mind!'"

Our teacher then said, "Well, those are good. But to me, a good meditation practice is one that you do."

She then explained how we have attachments to end results and that if we can't achieve those desired results, we'll judge ourselves and our efforts as bad and give up trying. She then added that even if you sit for 30 minutes and have absolutely no internal silence, that it's okay. We're building spiritual muscles, and those can take quite a while to get strong! I've been sitting about an hour a day an average of six days a week for well over a decade. And still, with all that practice, I often have no inner silence. But I don't self-criticize. I accept it and actually celebrate that I took that time for me. If "quiet-mind" is my goal, then I'm a failure. If taking personal time and as my Buddhist teacher explained, just doing it is my goal, then I'm a huge success.

Memory

The amount of memories we're conscious of is infinitesimal when compared to the total volume of the unconscious memories and the immense storage capacity of the human brain. Forgotten events, people, and feelings can resurface when triggered by healing modalities, familiar situations, music, or events that tend to repeat until we take notice.

Let's meet Henry, introduced to the public via the documentary *Alive Inside*. Henry was described as catatonic, but when he heard music from his past, his verbal abilities and memories came flooding back to him!

The narrator says: "We first see Henry inert, maybe depressed, unresponsive and almost un-alive . . . then he is given an iPod containing his favorite music and immediately he lights up. His face assumes expression, his eyes open wide, he starts to sing, to rock and to move his arms, and he's being animated by the music. . . . . When the headphones are taken off, Henry, normally mute and virtually unable to answer the simplest yes or no questions, is quite voluble."

How many of you can hear a song and know exactly where you were the first time you heard it? And perhaps more importantly, how many of you notice an energetic shift when remembering a specific song, even if it is decades later?

Many people feel that the brain's remarkable storage capacities can be kept intact, believing it to be similar to other muscles, in that usage creates strength. The phrase, "neurons that fire together wire together" mentioned in numerous books and documentaries echoes this idea. If this is taken to its next logical conclusion, we should exercise our brains as much as—or more than—we exercise our biceps. Maybe we should challenge ourselves more than we currently do, including learning more and being more active in life. So many of the elderly or even young retirees I've known are much happier and healthier when they're actively involved in life— when they have a sense of community, when they feel cared for and loved, and when they're curious about life and are genuinely grateful. Sadly, too many cultures disregard the elderly, but how much of that is a manifestation of our own fear of getting older, frail, and ill? Perhaps exercising the brain more often, thereby rewiring or forming new neural connections, can be helpful in preventing or minimizing memory failures.

Of course, due to the current pace of life, it's getting more and more difficult to maintain focus. There are countless shiny things and people vying for our attention or affection. Consciously choose where your attention is best utilized. Slow down, and listen for guidance to get you through overwhelming times. As you do your work, it may trigger the recollection of memories that have been buried for years, even decades. I recall a specific client who was able to "see" images from her childhood that explained her lifelong fears and challenges. The safe space I held for her let her access what she had to bury decades prior. Now, as an adult, her body felt it was time to show her the answers she'd been seeking.

Narcissists

At a recent lecture, I shared the qualities I understood to be descriptive of a narcissist. Admittedly, they were all negative. One attendee asked if there were positive aspects of narcissists, adding, "What about that they're hard-working, that they get things done?"

I said, "Yes, those can be positive, but it's about the underlying energy, even more than the intention or end result. If any action is done from fear—the subconscious MO (modus operandi) for the narcissist—or those actions gain followers or customers via manipulation or stepping on the backs of others, in the bigger picture that can only have negative end results."

Fear is the subconscious MO for narcissists?

Narcs, as I like to call them, often live in extreme fear of being found out that they're unintelligent and/or unpopular and/or unloved. So they lie, cheat, constantly distract, never take personal ownership, and manipulate others to give a projection of being more than they are.

The next question was about the narcissist breaking free of their own shackles.

I replied, "Trauma. Intense emotional distress can break the armor of the heart shield they've created. It can be their own trauma—an illness, for example—or that of someone close to them. I've yet to see or hear of any gentle ways of getting through."

In some ways, narcissism is like schizophrenia—an awfully painful period can't be managed and an alternate reality is created. They're individuals in severe mental and emotional pain, not bad people at their core. And they likely won't pursue any emotional healing because their egos have convinced them they're always correct, and always the victim never the cause. Hating them won't be effective for you or for them.

Why are we as Empaths and HSPs so adept at attracting narcissists into our lives?

Because we're feelers and healers, and no one needs us more than a narc. Many of us like to feel needed. We want to know that we're using our gifts, so we seek those in pain to help. But narcs only want us in their lives to fulfill their own perceived emptiness and needs. Too often we try to accommodate their needs to get the love we desire. But the love they give in return is conditional. If you've attracted a narc into your life, odds are high you've been in a similar situation before and that wound as yet is unhealed. If a parent, for example, is a narcissist, it can take years of breaking free of the shackles you've unconsciously kept yourself in. The newer person becomes the parent substitute.

Sadly, the desire to give and receive love outweighs the logical mind. Even if we're aware of the other person's shortcomings, the emotional connection is as strong as it is familiar, and many of us have to work diligently to break free of familiarity. Once we fully know we're not responsible for healing anyone, and/or learn that we've followed old, conditioned belief systems, we can make better choices. We can notice the draw, befriend it to reduce its pull, then not follow that enticement. Repeating this new pattern will eventually minimize the power of the old pattern and create newer and healthier neural pathways.

What we need to be is compassionate with a narc, which may not be easy at first! If we recognize that they're hurting and have no tools or conscious desire to admit to the existence of—or manage—their emotional pain productively, being compassionate will be easier.

Obesity

It is commonly believed that obesity is an end result of poor food choices combined with a sedentary lifestyle. While those certainly are important factors, they're just two-thirds of the equation. The third leg of the triad is our emotional state. Without addressing the buried emotions, a typically large part of the underlying cause is left unexamined and therefore, unhealed. This missing piece may explain the yoyo effect, or why weight loss is so difficult at all.

We learned early on that one way of dealing with unpleasant emotions was distraction via food. Because we replay the past, it's not uncommon for those I've worked with who are overweight to have buried numerous layers of emotional pain with food. This isn't much different from the alcoholic drinking to forget his problems and then still having the very same problems the very next day. Distraction doesn't work.

Instead, when you're upset and feel an urge to eat when already full, try letting yourself feel the emotion without judging it and eventually watching that emotion or discomfort dissolve via unconditional witnessing, as described in Chapters 4 and 6. Let your repeated trips to the kitchen and perhaps opening the refrigerator several times in a short period of time be a red flag that something is going on emotionally that you don't want to feel. With conscious awareness of this deeper truth, we can be with the craving and not have to fill its needs. It's not easy but nothing worth having or experiencing is.

As you may have already guessed, empaths and HSPs have the added burden of taking on the unhappy and/or unresolved emotions of others in addition to our own. Many of us who learned the food distraction game then try to calm those feelings with emotional eating. When the cravings arise, breathe, slow down your movements, and do the Body Scan, which will allow the information about what's going on to rise to the surface. When it does, follow the instructions in the Healing sections of *Empathipedia*.

I've often intuited that a more specific causative factor is that weight offers a form of protection for the person. If someone has had physical or emotional trauma, they might put on extra weight as a form of protection against potential victimizers. There is often an underlying fear of reoccurrence of the traumatic event(s). Especially in this case, one needs to be held in sacred space and allowed to feel, love, and heal those feelings of hopelessness, anxiety, and fear.

For many of us, our minds won't let us get to the required depth for deep healing if we try to do this on our own. The fear of feeling too much and/or being overwhelmed overrides the potential healing. In safe space, we're more likely to be able to access those heavier energies and emotions. I had one client say that she felt like she was going to die when intense fear arose within her. By challenging that belief while being held in sacred space, she was able to move through the discomfort and into a place of freedom.

Of course, there are other potential factors, but these are the ones I've seen the most and have had the most success with.

Parenting

"Dave, when my mommy is mad, I get sad!" said my six-year-old client.

"Tell me more" I replied.

"Dave, when my mommy is sad, I get mad!" he said.

"What else? I asked.

"Know what? I can feel the sadness of people 20 blocks away!"

I then said, "That's wonderful! But you don't need to. It's not your job to feel all that sadness. Know what else? Sadness isn't a bad thing. Your mommy and those people in other homes near you have to learn how to manage it."

"Oh, okay."

And that was it. My shortest session with my shortest client. He got it. First time.

His mother emailed me the next day explaining how different he'd been since the session. I think a big part of his turnaround was that I didn't make him wrong. I didn't address him as if he was broken. Other practitioners he'd gone to made him feel worse. I acknowledged what was true for him and let him know he was normal. That allowed him to trust me so that my "advice" was well received.

Kids want to know that they're loved and safe. They'll ask you for confirmation and validation in myriad ways. We can give them what they need.

Empathic children who pick up on the energy of their environment and caretakers need to know their caretakers are okay; otherwise, they'll absorb energies in an attempt to heal, connect or to give and receive love. If they get any sense that absorbing makes others feel better, they'll continue, sometimes throughout their entire lives.

Conscious parenting has to include individual awareness, growth, and authenticity. If a parent is feeling sad, they should verbalize that they're sad and that it's okay that they're sad. If a parent stoically tells a child they're okay when they're actually very sad, children can feel right through that lie. Duplicity is learned, and trust is reduced. If we know and share what's true for us and also reassure them that even if we're having difficulty we will be okay or are seeking help, they'll be less likely to absorb our energies. Parenting is about modeling. If we model integrity and honesty, we teach children to do the same.

Past Lifetimes

Past lifetimes can show up in a reading, but so will the current lifetime's re-creation of that prior experience. While I'm open to past lifetimes, my work is on healing and empowerment, and focusing on the present lifetime is more tangible and therefore more empowering.

For example, if betrayal was a major part of your prior lifetimes, it'll show up again in this one. And if forgiveness work has to be done, what's more accessible: retrieving memories to forgive someone you never met or forgiving someone you know pretty well? Interestingly, they may be the same person!

Predictions

One of my clients told me that not one but two renowned psychics told her that grieving the breakup of an intimate relationship takes seven years for a woman . . . and 30 days for a man.

I asked her if she'd ever heard of a doctor giving someone six months to live only to later see that person perish in just six weeks, or another person with the same prognosis who was still here six years later. Her answer was, of course, yes.

I then asked her what would these two psychics say about a same-sex relationship? Perhaps two biological women, where one shows more of her masculine side, and the other more her feminine side. Which wins—biology or sexual essence? Which woman gets to grieve for 30 days and which one has to wait seven years? Or two biological men who are both highly in their feminine energy? Are they both doomed to grieving longer than it takes to pay off a car, or are they ready to start dating again at the next full moon? And more importantly, what if any one person—regardless of biology, sexual essence, or sexual orientation—were highly aware of a healthy grieving process and another was taught to remain stoic?

It saddens me that good-intentioned people—medical doctors or psychics or other—can throw these numbers out so nonchalantly without taking any of the above and so much more into consideration.

Maybe it's fun to hear your local psychic say, "You're going to meet the man of your dreams in June" or "I am seeing you stepping into financial abundance," and who knows, maybe by hearing that, the listener might be more inclined to take action steps to make those predictions come true. Or maybe they'd hear those words and decide not to do anything to create this better future, thinking it's already in the cards. So many variables. Either way, I'd listen to any prognostication with the proverbial grain of sea salt.

When a (potential) client asks me, "How long do you think it will take for results to manifest when doing this work with you?" my answer is, "If anyone answers that, I'd recommend running the other way."

I just don't think playing psychic games with someone's health serves me or them. I'd much rather dive into the work we need to do without specific expectations of time and open up to the realm of all possibilities. This is much easier to do if you believe that the Universe wants you to heal. More accurately, my experience has shown me that the Universe wants us to learn something, and if healing happens as a side effect or part of the main intention, all the better.

If we address blockages, pain, or illness with the perhaps oxymoronic "logical and intuitive" steps, only good things can occur. If we are willing to face our inner shadow, or whatever arises as the cause of the condition while doing the inquisitive aspect of the healing work, symptoms can be reduced or eliminated. But they'll do so when we've done our work. No magic pill or generic energy healing work will address the cause on its own. Even surgery, though often necessary, at least energetically, is adding more trauma to existent trauma. We have to unearth the deeper layers of the affliction and work with them directly—regardless of physical steps taken or left on the table.

And we'll be done when we are done.

Public Speaking

If we are in touch with our gifts but can't share them with anyone, what good is having those gifts? For those who want to share their gifts as a business, we have to be able to market our services effectively. We must do so without coming from fear or greed, but rather from a heartfelt desire to serve. That's especially true if our target market is sensitives or intuitives, as they'll see right through you and can tell if you're coming from fear or if you're in your heart! Ideally, by putting yourself out there without attachments, others will feel your integrity. If it's obvious that you are living what you're preaching they'll be more inclined to work with (or buy from) you.

As much as we'd like to make a sale or share a gift, not everyone will want to work with you. We should accept this potential rejection as much as the potential "Yes!"

To market on a bigger scale and to gain the trust of more persons, you may need to speak to a room filled with people.

Oh no, not public speaking! Anything but that!

Don't worry. Just think of them as enemies who are judging your every word, movement, even your clothing! I'm only partially joking. They will be judging you. That's human nature. But they're not your enemies. Public speaking may or may not be part of your path. If it is, let me share with you how this formerly highly introverted child and adult who never liked crowds was able to stay calm and present in front of several thousand onlookers judging—um, I mean, listening to—me.

After the success of my first book and lots of positive feedback about several smaller events I'd led in New York City, I was asked to share the lecture bill with Deepak Chopra. I was excited and scared out of my mind! I spent the morning of the event trying to listen to Dr. Chopra and a few other speakers, but I couldn't take any of it in. I was in fear because I had no script to work from. I had no clue how I'd be received by what I perceived to be "his room." Somehow, I trusted things would be okay, yet I was still beyond nervous!

When they finally announced my name, I approached the stage—knees slightly wobbling—and a little voice pierced my fear. "It's not about you."

These four tiny yet magical words brought me out of my mind filled with fear and into my body. I realized that every fear I had was about me: If I stumbled, mumbled, lost my train of thought, or even fell, what would they think of me? What if they didn't like me? What if they disagreed with my message? What if they didn't like my hair (or what's left of it!). Me, me, me.

When I let the four-word message sink in, I realized I could be the most natural version of myself. I could be goofy and informative, and how I was perceived had nothing to do with me but rather the projections of those listening. To paraphrase the common vernacular, "What they think of me is none of my business." I had a blast and was well received. Over a year later, a random person approached me and told me that he had attended that event. He then paraphrased what I'd said on stage about forgiveness, adding how powerful that had been for him! For a relative newcomer to the field, that was an incredible feeling.

There were other defining moments that helped me get over my stage fright. Many years prior, after watching a chiropractor speak to a room with only about a dozen attendees I asked, "How can you speak to *all* those people like that?" He replied, "It's easy. I'm talking about what I love."

As paid experts, we are expected to know a lot. And often times we do. But on occasion you may be asked something you're not sure of. Do you muddle through it? Do you make something up? Or as most people do, distract from the original question with a pivot. I now see it's preferable to say, "Great question. I don't know the answer to that. Can I research it a bit and get back to you?" or quite simply, "I don't have enough experience in that area to give you a proper answer." Honesty and humility will get you very far, and perhaps as importantly, free you up to present the best possible version of you to your room!

And one more thing, get over the possibility or the fact that others may have done or said what you're about to share. There is only one you, and your delivery may be the one that gets through to a person. I heard Louise Hay say to the audience at one of her weekends featuring the biggest names in the business, "You're about to hear the same thing from 12 different authors. Hopefully, one of them gets through to you." Your understanding, experience, and embodiment make your delivery a true one of a kind!

Quantum Physics

If you think you understand quantum mechanics, you don't understand quantum mechanics.

–Richard Feynman, theoretical physicist

Relationships

It often seems that most adults are chasing any or all of the following: intimate relationships, vibrant health, and financial prosperity. Amazingly (to me at least), none of these are taught in traditional schooling. And maybe, just maybe, that's why so many adults I work with are having challenges in at least one (and sometimes more) of these areas.

As far as intimate relationships are concerned, my own circuitous 30 years of serial dating were filled with, *Gotta find the right one . . . NOW!* Anyone else relate to that? I chased, sought, ran to, and ran from every conceivable way of meeting the perfect partner, believing as Steve Martin's character in *LA Story* said, "There's someone out there for everyone—even if you need a pickaxe, a compass, and night goggles to find them."

In retrospect, I can see that each relationship taught me something invaluable, and that the reason so many ended was because of my numerous unrealistic expectations. When those expectations weren't met, I focused on what I perceived as the follies of my intimate partners and blamed them for things not working out. When I finally owned up to my own part in all of that during a conversation at a Thai restaurant, tears rained down into my Pad See Yew. I committed in that moment to open my heart and also to question my mind's ideas of how my partner should or shouldn't look, be, act, and so on.

Eventually I saw that those fantasies were projections of my own insecurities of how I should or shouldn't look, be, and act, learned from what culture, conditioning, and the media were portraying. My relationships were a giant "should-be." Like most of us, I learned what to do and what not to do via trial-error-repeat-correct and heartbreaking experience after heart-opening experience.

Over the next few years, I practiced catching any old patterns, blessing them, then inviting in a new thought with more consistency and more tenacity. And it worked! That led me to the realization that there was another path: surrender. I intuited that Source enjoys being the cupid of dating and dared myself to allow the process rather than force it.

I set an intention to find a complement rather than someone who I would perceive to complete me, and the Universe sent me my wife, Maria. And while no pickaxe was necessary, it did take moving 3,000 miles away based on a vision I repeatedly saw in a meditation that had nothing specifically to do with her! And then joining Match(dot)com in the new city and meeting an amazing person who I didn't date but rather became great friends with who knew a guy who invited us both to his house where I met his friend, Maria. Simple, right? Remember that straight line thing? Not!

I share the above to hopefully inspire you that if you are patient and follow guidance, Source will always connect you with someone perfectly aligned for you!

Sometimes, a client asks me to help them find the perfect partner. While I could conceivably intuit where they should go, what they should do, and so on, when we go deeper I hear that I should remind them to focus on themselves first—relationship prep! By working on ourselves, practicing presence and nonreactivity, and by improving our listening skills and authentic communication abilities, we create the internal conditions that are received by others—including the person you're supposed to meet no matter where they are!

What is your intention in a relationship? Some people may not want to be alone. Some may want a teammate for events or TV watching. Some just want sex. Some may only want someone to cook for them. Some may want to stay home and nurture youngsters or cats while their partner is making a living outside the home. Others may want a trophy to be seen with. None of these are bad intentions in and of themselves; however, for empaths and HSPs and many on a path of deeper exploration, most of the above will leave us feeling unfulfilled.

At our deepest core, I believe we all want to grow and expand, and relationships are an amazing vehicle for that to happen. If your goal is expansion into deeper levels of love, both parties have to be willing to do their own work. As issues arise—and they will if you're doing it well—there are supportive ways of telling your partner what you see and feel. Each party should commit to holding safe space for sharing fears and insecurities, desires and fantasies.

Sometimes we have to be willing to take a chance on upsetting someone. Ironically, as a male in the USA and having learned that I needed to be tough and emotionally resilient (resistant), I've found others trust me more when I challenge my own belief systems and become soft in the heart and vulnerable with my words. And I allow and even invite others to share what's true for them, even if what's said upsets me. If the words of another person trigger an upset, I look at why it upsets me rather than making my partner wrong for stirring up my emotions. Relationships are potentially a daily exercise routine in self-awareness and response.

When clients tell me of their partner's idiosyncrasies and look to something outside the self for their happiness, I have to tell them that, barring self-destructive or abusive situations, what others are doing matters little. What matters is our response to what they are doing or saying or how they are.

Slow down and ask yourself, "How do I choose to be in relationship with what is arising inside or outside of me?" Then breathe and await intuitive guidance. Or use logic to remind yourself of what's true and what's not, then weigh the options on how best to respond. Over time, this gets easier. And it is so worth the effort!

I once listened to Lama Ole Nydahl talk about losing his wife after her long bout with illness. He described how horrifically painful it was for both of them. Someone asked him, "Knowing what you know now, and how painful that was, what advice can you share about an intimate relationship?" And without any thought at all, he smiled and said, "It's worth it."

Shadow

According to Jungian philosophy, and that of many others wiser than me, we all have the potential to act in every way possible. (If you disagree, look up the Stanford Prison Experiment.) I visualize this range numerically on a scale of zero to 100, where zero is a complete shutdown of the heart's love, leaving someone willing to hurt or kill others, and 100 being pure, unconditional love. Most of us typically operate between 40 and 60. When we're in a me-pression, for example, we might be at a 30. When we're in a rage, that might be closer to 15, and so on.

Those lower numbers represent our unintegrated pain that is housed within what is often referred to as our "shadow," partly because it doesn't want to be seen. Even if we're aware that we have a shadow, we typically don't want others to see it. Heck, most of us don't even want to see the shadow within ourselves!

Denying the shadow increases its energy and manifests in numerous ways—for example, a guy who rants and raves against prostitution and is later caught with a prostitute; someone who paints a squeaky-clean image and is later found guilty of larceny, or worse; or the person claiming his disgust of same-sex relationships who is later found with a same-sex partner.

But it's not only those we deem deceitful or hypocritical who act out their shadow energies. Who here hasn't hurt another person, even though our intentions may have been positive? Who among us has never acted out from our unconscious patterns? We are all in the same boat, and the boat has an upper and a lower portion, but both are still parts of the same boat! A boat without a top portion that exists above the water surface is a barge, and a taller boat without the lower portion made for submergence won't float. Similarly, a person who has yet to acknowledge their shadow aspect will rarely feel complete, nor can they face the shadows in others and offer high levels of love and compassion.

It can be said that the unintegrated shadow is at least partly responsible for the ills of man—inclusive of economic inequality, abuse of power, misunderstanding and misappropriation of sexual energy, and wars. Those who identify with certain aspects of shadow live in poverty consciousness, believing that there is never enough of whatever they desire. This fear manifests outward as greed.

Trying to reason with someone weighed down by the fear aspect of their shadow typically doesn't go well if they've become deeply identified with that aspect. What isn't integrated, accepted, and honored is identified by the shadow as an identity. The ego will defend its identity and will not let the person see that their fear is illogical. You can show someone who is entrenched in fear the statistics that back up your claim that, for example, the odds on a plane taking off and landing intact are dramatically higher than the odds of it crashing, but the person in fear will find a way to justify their position, discredit the obvious information, or even discredit you.

As we get closer to the inevitable tipping point where the majority of people realize we're all connected, shadow elements, both inside and outside of us that are identified with separation will flare up with greater intensity and frequency. As the shadow self becomes more exposed in society or those closest to us, the unintegrated aspects of our own shadow will be triggered. Judging other people for acting from their shadow shows us that we haven't integrated those shadow aspects, either! Integrating the shadow heals it and allows us to operate from love rather than fear with increased and increasing frequency.

We're not responsible for healing the shadow in others but freeing ourselves from the grip of our own shadow can only have a positive effect on the whole. To quote Marianne Williamson, ". . . as we let our own light shine, we unconsciously give other people permission to do the same. As we are liberated from our own fear, our presence automatically liberates others."

T'nnitus

I've worked with quite a few clients of late who were suffering from ringing in the ear, or what they had been told was tinnitus. In each case, I have intuited a prolonged repression of grief energy.

Grief can be held deep within the body for years, even decades, before the ringing symptoms arise. Because it is so deeply embedded, it's more difficult to access on one's own, but that doesn't mean it's impossible. Accessing deeper layers of grief often takes time, patience, and willingness to witness unpleasant emotions within, but the journey is well worth it!

In these and many other cases with deeply engrained energies, it's important to know that even a small "chipping away of the stone" is a positive thing. Just like carving a statue, a healed place already exists within us, we need to chip away the barriers that have prevented healing taking place. As we work with, uncover, and heal repressed grief, symptoms can be healed at the root level.

Throat Issues

We all want to feel seen and heard. Communication is how we get our needs met, express love and concerns, and oftentimes, heal.

Among the clients I've worked with who have had any kind of issues in the throat, most if not all have not felt seen or heard. Their communication skills had been stifled. They lacked freedom of expression. They feel constantly evaluated by others and feel they have to watch what they say, how they say it, and to whom.

The body's chakras are vortexes where energy can flow in and out, and a closed chakra is the result of a lack of energetic flow. By working to restore the flow of energy through that chakra, the blockage will be healed. The throat chakra is all about communication, and as such, many of the problems associated with that area result from communication breakdowns. It makes sense, therefore, that in addition to other healing modalities, we should improve our communication.

Today, vulnerability and authenticity in our daily interactions are emerging as a powerful force. It makes sense, therefore, that we can take this one step farther and open a closed chakra by challenging ourselves to speak our truth, regardless of who is listening. Ideally, we don't speak our truth to convince others of our correctness, level of knowledge, or a desire to look good; rather, we use it to share words of compassion and love to those currently in need, and to those from our past.

If we have unfinished business with someone, we should clean that up whenever possible. When verbal communication isn't possible, we can visualize and then speak to that person's higher self. If that proves difficult, we can use a picture of that person. Though it'll feel odd at best, just speaking out loud can have healing effects—even more so if a friend or trusted practitioner can witness this one-way exchange.

Often, just by beginning to speak subtle truths, momentum will build and deeper layers will become more accessible. It may feel wrong to voice our fears or our perceived failures, but in order to heal we must not only access and speak them but also befriend them. Having our grievances, anger, or sadness seen and heard by others who accept these as part of the human condition can dissipate the blockage, catalyze flow and healthy innervation, and aid in symptom reduction and eradication.

Movement, music, or art, can be also powerful methods of communication. For many of us, they are the way in, a way of communicating that accesses and communicates important truths and understandings in a deeply personal way by bypassing the mental blocks that keep us stuck. Have you ever been moved by a dance performance or a piece of music, literature, or art? When I saw Vincent van Gogh's painting, "Starry Night" in person—after seeing it perhaps dozens of times in print—I was brought to tears. I felt the sadness of the man through his art, more than 120 years after its creation! I can't imagine how much worse his emotional state would have been without his creative expression.

Dare yourself to communicate only truth. What may initially seem scary, can also be a ticket to freedom, or at minimum, your throat chakra opening!

Uncertainty

We want to know that any path we pursue—whether it be healing an ailment or painting a picture—will turn out well. We don't want to waste time trying things out; rather, we want to be certain something will be worth our time and effort. But in metaphysics or in energy medicine, no outcome is certain.

The mind hates this, but the fact is, we live with uncertainty all the time. We often don't know what a new dish will taste like until we take a bite. We don't know what condition other drivers are in, but we still get in our cars and drive. We don't know for sure what other people are thinking, but we associate with them anyway. While the degrees of safety are in our favor in these instances and many others, certainty of an outcome is rarely 100 percent. Even surgeries scientifically proven to be effective don't have a 100 percent success rate. There are just too many variables to ever be certain about anything. But we don't let that stop us from living. Ideally, anyway.

Countless times, I've heard people say, "But I've done so much work. . .". While it's understandable that frustration can creep in after years or even decades of working to get better at something—health included—the phrase, "But I've done so much work. . ." indicates a lack of acceptance of uncertainty. Those who speak this generally believe that if only they did A, B, and C, they'd be healed or even enlightened but have been shattered by the reality of continued symptoms, loneliness, or lack of abundance. An expectation hasn't been met.

In the macrocosm, or the physical universe, unless you're a slacker, it's a given that if you go to college for four years, odds are high that you'll graduate with some kind of degree. But in the microcosm, or the quantum universe, nothing is guaranteed. When we apply the understandings of either the microcosm or macrocosm to the other, misery is often the end result—meaning, don't count on gaining your Spiritual PhD even if you've been working at something for years, decades, or even lifetimes.

To have any semblance of inner peace, it's vital to understand that nothing in the microcosm is certain, no matter how hard one tries. If we accept our journey's inevitable ups and downs and the circuitous routes to healing, abundance, or any desired outcome, we'll have more joy along the way.

As intuitives, we expect clear answers whenever we want them. But as you already know, that's not always the case, especially when doing self-readings. Our state of mind affects the intuition and thus, the degree of certainty. One of the few things I can be 100 percent certain of is that whenever I calm myself, my intuition guides me well. Maybe not right away or directly, but eventually and in a manner that is necessary for my growth. I can let that frustrate me, or I can embrace the uncertainty for what it is—an inescapable aspect of daily life.

Validation

I think we all seek validation from family members, peers, romantic partners, even employers. We developed our identity based on how others saw and acknowledged us (or didn't), and we often spend much of our lives proving them right—for better or worse.

While that is typical, it's not always healthy. Seeking external validation is giving away our power. We need to access the creative power within to make better decisions, which may be the exact opposite of what we've been conditioned to believe or do. The deeper growth comes from loving ourselves through our failures and weaknesses—loving all aspects of ourselves and others— proverbial warts and all, regardless of validation received or denied.

Can you imagine the freedom associated with not needing external validation? Spiritual masters inhabit this state. When we witness them, we are inspired by their personal freedom, their liberation from egoistic attachments and external validation. They know that we are all perfect as we are, and even our imperfections are perfect! If you've ever loved another person unconditionally or been loved by someone unconditionally, you have experienced this juicy state of being. Part of our journey is accessing this internal state more often. From an inner knowing of what is true and what isn't, we may still enjoy external validation, but the need for it is superfluous.

Weapons of Mass Distraction

I can't even begin to count the number of times I've saved the work you're reading now and flipped over to check my email or see what's up on Facebook! If I had my phone nearby, no doubt I'd be receiving text messages and hearing assorted *bings* and *bongs* indicating that I've got an email, my virtual chess buddy just put me in check, or that an app needs an update.

These things have become so commonplace it's hard to remember what life was like without the constant barrage of distractions. As if that's not enough, the consistency of this fast-paced digital world has affected the mind's ability to stay focused, making everything we do more difficult and more time consuming. So many of us now are addicted to external satisfaction that internal peace has become the last thing we strive for! We prioritize texting, answering emails, scrolling through feeds of news or pictures of friend's dinners, or anything else that is external to the inner environment. Isn't it amazing that we know that a relaxed inner landscape is the precursor to better health and satisfaction in all areas, yet still we put it off till last, or not at all?

Other weapons of mass distraction include food and alcohol, even relationships, which when not utilized for our highest good can be a form of distraction. What are we all running from? What is it that so many of us are not willing to deal with that makes these distractions seem so enticing?

In my experience, pain from our past is always nagging us for integration. Empaths and HSPs are also bombarded with the unintegrated emotional aspects of people we know, and even those we don't, from both the past and the present. Other than that, this is easy. Ahem.

Willingness

A woman came to see me who was very stuck in her old ways. She resisted everything I said to her. Growing more frustrated with my suggestions, she eventually demanded, "WHY WON'T YOU HEAL ME?" I had to tell her that a) It's not that I'm unwilling; rather, it's that I'm unable to and b) I am not the one who does the healing.

Another way of putting it came to me shortly after she left. (Don't you hate it when that happens?) In retrospect I might have asked, "What makes you think that I can do what you've already indicated none of the dozens of practitioners you've seen have also been unable to do?" The commonality is that she was the only one there in each instance. Her adherence in being the emotional sponge was an addiction she wasn't willing to break.

One of my mentors said that willingness is the cosmic grease of healing. Without willingness to step into a new way of being, little change will happen at a deep level. There may be snippets of change or bits of symptom reduction, but deep transformation takes a desire to grow beyond one's comfort zone.

Sometimes we don't know what the body is willing to shift until we give it a try, so despite what Yoda said, try! If resistance arises, try to imagine what being on the other side of resistance looks and feels like. Sometimes this vision of more freedom or symptom reduction can increase the body's willingness so that deeper work can be done. One of the best tools I've seen to increase willingness is to physically list both the benefits and drawbacks of the old pattern as well as the benefits and drawbacks of the potential way of being. Handwriting this list, as opposed to thinking about or typing it, engages the mind in a more experiential way. Often, the body will feel the potential of the new expanded state of being and gets excited by the possibility. Cultivating willingness to get through the resistance paves the way toward more health and healing.

Worthiness

"I'm not worthy."

Besides this being a punchline for a *Wayne's World* skit, it's become a belief system to explain why any one of us isn't healing, abundant, or experiencing the life of our dreams.

Guess what? In my experience, no one feels worthy. I've worked with and heard about people who seem to have everything they possibly could desire, and you know what? They often feel unworthy, too.

So let's establish firmly that feeling unworthy is the norm, not the exception. It is part of the collective dream that we tap into and, in my opinion, spend too much time perpetuating as the reason why we're not feeling whole. I invite you to accept that unworthiness is part of the human condition.

I've actually embraced my own unworthiness. As I look at my amazing relationship, for example, I don't feel worthy of her. Professionally, I don't feel worthy of getting paid for what I do. And yet, here I am in this relationship. Here I am self-employed now for well over a decade without a "day job." So, my wife and clients feel I am worthy, regardless of my personal doubts.

I've decided not to give the subconscious loop of unworthiness much validity. Maybe we can all start dancing with doubt because it doesn't matter if we feel worthy or not. Spirit knows you are worthy so it will provide you with the opportunities to co-create and experience what you came here for!

Xtrovert

Yes, I know. I took creative spelling license. As per thefreedictionary(dot)com, an extrovert is both an outgoing person (rare for Empaths and HSPs) and also "a person concerned more with external reality than inner feelings," which describes the turmoil so many of us face. We have such intense inner feelings that we tend to distract ourselves and focus on what's external. We try to keep the peace out there when the real challenge is to keep the peace within. We can get caught up in what others are doing or saying and too easily forget that the thing that matters most is how we are being.

Though we are all connected, our mission is an individual one in a group experience. Ideally, we remind ourselves that as we heal ourselves, we also heal the collective that appears to be outside of us.

Yes!

A wonderful friend of mine is a powerful, beautiful woman who is creative, financially successful, funny, and gregarious. And she has had difficult relationship after difficult relationship. I sent her the Facebook profile of someone who lives in my neighborhood and asked if she would be interested in meeting him. At first she declined, but I intuited to invite her to think about it some more. I asked, "What would be the worst thing that could happen by meeting him in a coffee shop?"

A few days later she said she would be open to meeting him. At that time, I revisited his profile page and was struck with, "There is no way this is going to work out." I told her this, and she naturally asked, "Why did you think we'd vibe initially?" I didn't have an answer, so I went within. I intuited, then shared, "The Universe needed to hear you say 'yes' to doing something different." Not long thereafter she did connect with someone she could truly connect with.

Turns out the Universe wants us to be in YES mode. It wants us to open up to new possibilities. Sure, this was a roundabout way of getting her on board, but so what? If everything was too direct, what fun would that be?

Another way of looking at this is that the Universe is always saying yes to us. It knows what we need and when, and how to send that person, opportunity, or inspiration that will bring us to more of ourselves. All we have to do is say yes to the opportunity and then follow guidance on how to make it happen.

Zzzzzzzzzz's (Sleep Disorders)

Sleeping pills, blindfolds, background music, prayer, counting sheep, herbal supplements, essential oils, foods with high levels of tryptophan, imagery, feng shui—they all may help, but how many of them get to the underlying cause of your sleep challenges? All of these and many more temporary fixes can help in the short term, but too many short-term solutions can leave you just as tired upon awakening as you were before going to bed.

In my experience and understanding, most sleep or nighttime difficulties—barring those from physical challenges—are from unprocessed daytime emotions and/or unhealthy anticipation of a future event. It should make sense that if you haven't processed the emotions that arose during the day, your mind will keep you up or awaken you prematurely to try to process them when you slow down at night. Taken to the next logical step, what if months or even years of unprocessed emotions are left unprocessed? Chronic sleep disorders!

It's time to process.

All of my past? That could take forever!

Unlikely, because what isn't processed repeats itself, giving you numerous opportunities to heal an old pattern. It's the reactionary emotion that needs to be healed, not each and every event. Sometimes processing the emotions associated with only a few events can clear out years of backlog!

Processing means to feel the emotions that have been buried. For example, unprocessed grief from the early death of a loved one can and will be painful, but freedom and dramatically improved sleep are on the other side of that. There is no escaping and healing; there is only continued burying or denying or active feeling and processing.

But feeling and healing needn't be super painful. If you can get past the judgment of your most raw, human emotions, they can be processed and moved through relatively quickly.

When anxious about an upcoming event, the mind can run through countless potential scenarios. Because we learned to focus on the negative, most of those scenarios won't be pleasant. How often have you anticipated a worst-case scenario, and then the event came, and it wasn't nearly as bad as predicted? Prepping for an extremely difficult experience isn't always a negative thing, but incessantly repeating that preparation can be an unhealthy thing. Ideally, we take that preparation into the emotional realm and allow any and all feelings that arise when thinking about an upcoming event. From a post-emotional place, we can open to all possibilities and take logical steps to increasing the odds on a positive outcome. Next we should bring ourselves to the present moment and consciously choose our next course of action.

If upon awaking in the morning, you *need* coffee or other artificial stimulants (for example, sugary breakfast cereals) to get you going, something is out of balance. This can be an indication of sleep challenges, which as mentioned above is more of an unprocessed daytime events challenge. Do you see the vicious cycle here? If you do the work, you'll get better sleep and reduce or eliminate the need for artificial energy enhancers.

Who decided you need eight hours of sleep per night? And worse, why do you believe them? Do you know the persons who did the research? Did they ask you specifically, or a bunch of other people who could have entirely different health conditions and needs?

Worrying about getting the recommended eight hours of sleep is just one more thing for the mind to ruminate upon, keeping you from getting quality rest for fear of not getting enough rest! Another vicious cycle! I've found that focusing on the quality of sleep more than the quantity has brought me to a place where I can fall asleep easily, usually within a few minutes, and wake up ready to take on the day. I've noticed this to be true, whether I get five hours or nine hours of total sleep.

If you're in a rut of doing the same things each day, how much desire is there to get up when the alarm clock rings? Do you curse the alarm and imagine the dread you'll feel when you get to work? Or the frustration you'll experience when trying to make your point at an upcoming meeting? Conversely, what if you are excited by your upcoming day? What if you are truly feeling grateful for the known and unknown opportunities that await you? Don't you think that lifestyle will get you up and going with more energy and a smile rather than feeling the drudgery of same old, same old?

When we are busy doing things we love, socializing with people who understand us and that we enjoy, we bring a different energy to life and to sleep. There is less tension and anxiety in our mind and body, allowing us to fall asleep easily and to wake refreshed.

Of course, empaths and HSPs often hold the challenges of those closest to us and even the collective, in addition to our own tasks! How could we possibly get any high-quality sleep if our mind and/ or our body are busy managing the absorbed emotions of others!

Which brings us to our next section. . .

4

The Body Scan

Throughout history, people have spent time, money, energy, and resources trying to understand the nature of health and illness. We've run the gamut, from superstition to modern science, and have had miraculous success in extending lifespan along the way. Sadly, however, there has been more focus on symptom eradication than on prevention. And while there's nothing inherently wrong about wanting to feel better, the steps we've taken to feel better often preclude the truth that is trying to emerge within the symptoms.

If pain and illness are here to inform us that something we're doing or a particular way we're being is out of alignment with our highest and most connected selves, it's better to ascertain what those messages are and then reverse the direction we're going accordingly.

But how can we ascertain the hidden meanings within our symptoms? How can we always know what our bodies are trying to say?

We need to go beyond the mind to access our body's intelligence. The Body Scan is the description I was given to describe this process. It is different from the body scan relaxation technique that many of you may be familiar with, as it is specifically tailored to empaths and HSPs and allows us to see what's really going on, why the symptom or blockage is there, whose it is, and how to heal it. It has proven itself to be remarkably effective. When we sit with our symptoms rather than trying to push them away or bury them, we create space for a new awareness to arise. An inquiry of what exists creates a map for what can be. The Body Scan is an exercise in allowing what exists to exist, trusting that it does so to inform us rather than to hinder us.

Presence Activation Sequence

The ability to get past conditioned beliefs and into the core of our being is activated through present-moment awareness. One great way to achieve presence is to engage your physical senses. Try the below Presence Activation Sequence or any known grounding exercises that have proven effective for you before beginning the Body Scan.

Sit in a reasonably comfortable position, ideally not on a chair or couch with a back. Somewhat like meditation, we need to minimize the chances of falling asleep as a distraction.

1. Take a few conscious breaths, and look around the room. Make a mental note or say out loud what you see as the light reflects through the window, creating shadows that may be unique to that time of day. Just notice this or other things without adding any stories, or any "should-be" or "shouldn't be." Accept everything that is visible to you in that moment.

2. Take a few more conscious breaths, and close your eyes. Tune in to any sounds outside of the room you're in. Just notice what's there without any judgment. Stay with that awareness for a bit. Now tune into any sounds that are in the room you're in. Once again, just notice, without adding a story to them.

3. Tune in to any smells, or lack thereof. Notice. Observe. Stay with that awareness for a while. When the mind drifts, just bring your attention back to the sense of smell.

4. Now bring your awareness to your mouth. Any leftover tastes from a previous meal? A taste of toothpaste, perhaps? Just notice that without attachment. Pieces of leftover broccoli don't need a story.

5. Bring your awareness to your fingertips. Touch the thumb to your first finger, thumb to middle finger, thumb to ring finger and then thumb to pinky. Observe temperature, pressure, smoothness, or roughness. You can even vocalize one syllable per finger touch, "Bo-dy scan time." Now place your left hand on your right shoulder. Next, place your right hand on your left shoulder. Now, give yourself a hug.

The Presence Activation sequence is a way of showing the Universe you mean business and are ready to intuit what needs to be known. Assuming this relaxes you more than annoys you, state a clear intention to see or feel or hear what is needed to come through. It could take several tries, somewhat like meditation. Eventually, the information will arise.

As we invite what is already there to rise to the level of conscious awareness, the discomfort can be painful enough to distract yourself away from the very pathway needed to be traveled. Fears will arise, and one possible reaction will be self-criticism: *I should be able to do this.*

But those are the mind's ideas about what should or shouldn't exist, not what actually does exist. It takes a great deal of courage and determination, and of course, a willingness to stay the course through the deterrents that may arise. Many people I've taught this to have had wonderful success, while others have been frustrated. To the former: congratulations; to the latter: fear not! I find it quite normal to have difficulty transcending the ideas arising in your mind and get into your core self; for most people, the road is just too scary to travel alone.

Those who feel blocked, stressed, and overwhelmed can have difficulty accessing their own body's intelligence. I, too, have had difficulty opening enough to clearly see what's going on at my deepest layers on my own. It's not wrong or bad and doesn't mean that I or they or you are unintelligent, unloving, or unspiritual; rather, it's often an end result of energetic overwhelm that minimizes our internal focus.

> *If we were meant to go at it alone, there'd be*
> *7 billion planets; one person each.*
> –unknown author

Working with a teammate or group can help us break through walls and even years of frustration like nothing else can. When team member(s) hold you in safe space, there is an energetic shift that can't be explained by Western medicine or science, but nevertheless is tangible. Sure, this may be asking a lot, and in some cases teamwork is impossible, but where there's a will there's a way. As much as many of us feel alone, there is always someone who will understand you, whether they're a paid practitioner or a friend who lives thousands of miles away.

Awareness of empathy and high sensitivity is rising faster than sea levels. There are countless articles, blogs, books, and gatherings online or in person that can be accessed. And most of those people will be happy to help, if only you would ask. If that sounds scary, ask yourself this: If a vulnerable person reached out to you, asking you to hold safe space for them, wouldn't you be honored that they had asked? I think the reverse is true as well. We're honoring others and even complimenting their abilities as a friend, healer, or lay person to be of assistance.

What is safe space? How do I create that? How can I invite others to hold that for me?

Glad you asked.

Safe Space

A good friend once asked, "Why are you funny?" Knowing her, I knew this was an invitation to learn something about myself. So instead of rushing to give a quick answer, I sat with her in silence, consciously resisting the urge to make another joke, and out of my mouth quite unexpectedly came, "Because if I wasn't, no one would like me."

Didn't see that one coming. Such is the value of safe space.

When done well, safe space can give us access to our thoughts and feelings beyond conscious awareness. We can recall individual events and emotions that may have been buried long ago or the deepest reasons why we do or don't do certain things.

Safe space serves as a container for unconditional love and acceptance for whoever is in front of you. No matter what anyone says or emotes, everything in safe space is sacred. A safe container for all of our humanity—proverbial warts and all—is a vital tool that increases the success of doing honest, inner work.

As a practitioner, I've learned that safe space can magnify our intuition or healing work. When a client feels trust, you may hear things like, "I've never told anyone this before, but. . ." Our job is not to judge. Who are we to judge, anyway?!? In a world where our shadow selves are so often shunned and fought and still quite often the victor, giving voice to these hidden aspects of ourselves can be very comforting and even healing. Often just voicing what's actually true within safely contained space can be a doorway to radical transformation. Self-acceptance can be elicited by external acceptance.

I worked with a woman who was talking about her employment and how she felt underused and undervalued. I could sense that there was something much more pressing that needed light and said, "I get how that is very important to you. I'm also sensing that there is something much deeper on your mind and heart." Because I said this without attachment or judgment, she immediately began to cry. By feeling beyond her story, I'd pierced her heart's protective armor enough for her to access and share a deeper and more relevant truth. After several minutes of tears, she told me about her relationship with her mom—how difficult that was and how that was affecting her. We did some work around that, and she felt lighter and free. But none of that would have happened without the safe container.

Even if you are being paid to be an energetic healer, healing another person is not your job. Your main job is to accept and love them unconditionally. This, quite ironically, can actually help them heal.

If you need to access a deeper part of yourself, you can ask someone to hold safe space for you. If they're unaware of what that is or its value, tell them that you're going to help each other heal. Who wouldn't get excited by that?

Tell them that you're going to sit together, ideally in silence and listen . . . really listen . . . as if your lives depended on what's being said. You're going to listen to the other person as if they're telling you the secret to all joy and healing. Assuming there are two of you, we'll call you and them Persons A and B, respectively.

Person A will be in the "hot seat," so to speak. Person B will read the Presence Activation Sequence in order to begin creating safe space. Person B is the unconditional witness to Person A. Person B should listen to what's being said and not verbalize anything in response. Nor do they need to empathize, or even nod their head in agreement.

This will be unsettling at first, as it goes against most, if not all, of our social norms. Do it, anyway. Person B agrees not to judge whatever is being said and agrees to keep whatever is said in that room. When the Presence Activation Sequence is complete, and Person A feels the safety of the container, they can begin the Body Scan.

The Body Scan

Set a clear intention to hear/see/feel information you normally can't access. Ask your body and/or the Universe to show you what is in need of attention in this moment. Person A should state any variant of, "I allow the needed information, answers, feelings, memories, symptoms, sounds, or smells to arise," and when what's asked for emerges, state it out loud.

Because the Universe wants you to learn, it will support you in this process. Try to allow it to unfold rather than force it. The answer may not come every time. Try to be okay with that, and just try again later. But in my extensive experience in doing this, well over 90 percent of clients say they can clearly access what needs to be addressed when I hold safe space. More often than not, attention is brought to a chakra, but it can also be your nose or your toes. Be open! Once you have the answer, tell your teammate what that is.

Now that you know which area is calling for some deeper work, ask your body to further the process. Inquire as to what energy or emotion is locked there. With patience, the answer will arrive. You may hear the word "grief," or if you're more visceral, you may begin to feel sad. You may sense anger as your body tightens, or you may remember a particular event from the past. You may experience a heaviness or see darkness.

Feel deeper into what's arising, and in the case of heaviness or darkness, open to the possibility that these sensations are visual or visceral representations of frustration, anxiety, or grief. It can also be a vague sensation, beyond words. That's okay; let it be there—especially knowing that you didn't just create this feeling, but rather, with your consciousness, you became more aware of what's already existing within you. That's what we're looking to heal—the hidden layers that were too painful for you to feel, which were buried long ago. Tell your teammate what you're witnessing or feeling.

Now for the all-important question, "Is this mine, someone else's, or a combination?" Let the information come to you. You may see it, feel it, hear it, or just know it. Once you have the answer, tell your teammate what that answer is.

You now have information you likely didn't have even a few minutes ago. You will have the area in need of attention, what type of energy or emotion is blocked there and creating the symptoms, and whose it is! With this awareness, you can now begin the deeper healing processes designed specifically for empaths and HSPs.

5

Healing What's Been Absorbed Using "Return to Sender"

Using the information gathered in the Body Scan, described in Chapter 4, you can now begin healing what ails you at the root level.

The repressed energy you're now consciously aware of has either been empathically absorbed or it's your own. There are no other choices. If it belongs to others, we have to give the energy back to them using a process I intuited to call "Return to Sender." Apparently, that's not just the name of an awesome Elvis Presley song. If what's been revealed is yours, it must be integrated. That is discussed in Chapter 6.

Let's say, for example, you've just determined that you've empathically absorbed your mother's grief and have been storing it in your heart chakra. You have to give that energy back to her.

Why would I want to do this? Couldn't I just transform it for her?

No.

Why not?

Because despite your best of intentions, holding or healing energies that belong to another person, relevant or irrelevant to your relationship with that person, doesn't serve you. Nor does it serve the other person.

Each person arrives here with a soul's mission. The soul doesn't judge any aspects of that mission; we do. Who are we to judge or even assume what another soul came here for? This isn't meant to sound callous or mean; rather, it's an invitation to step beyond our conditioned belief systems into something vaster. A heightened awareness of soul-level needs is crucial to the effectiveness of this work.

No other person can truly heal you; however, the Universe helps those who help themselves. So we each have to step it up a bit for true healing to occur. A big part of that is accepting this new reality—you're an emotional sponge, and you needn't be.

In the above example, holding onto your mother's grief is the causal level of what you've been calling fatigue, heartache, or any of the myriad of ways that repressed grief can manifest. Mom's grief is her very natural healing response to any type of loss, so why would we want to take that away? Removing her underlying grief, and thus her awareness that it needs healing, is like clipping the wires on the dashboard light while the engine is overheating. Taking away another person's grieving process can even be likened to removing part of their immune system.

Your mom may have had a difficult life, and although holding her energy may seem helpful, it's actually holding her back. She needs to have what's hers in order to heal it. If you are holding onto what's hers, she cannot be aware of what's needed and will have less incentive to manage the loss.

None of this means we should hold less compassion for her. In fact, it's more compassionate to love her unconditionally and not only accept her soul's mission, but in this case, help it along by giving back to her what is inherently hers to manage. We can, of course, be there for her. We can talk with her, hug her, and let her know she is loved. We could even recommend a book or supplement or practice, but ideally, we should do so without attachment (no matter how difficult that may be), because that is what is best for all.

Whether she does that inner work or not, it is still important to give her back what's hers. What we're really doing is helping her return to a place of wholeness. By us holding a piece of her energy, she isn't whole, and in addition, we are weighed down with what's hers.

In one of my favorite analogies, imagine a beautiful painting of a lake on a partly sunny day. The top third of the painting shows the clouds and lots of blue sky lit by the sun. The middle third of the painting is the water. The bottom third is darkness, representing all the things under the surface that we typically can't see. If grief is buried in the darkness and we remove it, as one might remove a piece of a jigsaw puzzle, there is emptiness in the middle of that darkness. The whole image is ruined. It's no longer metaphorically complete and illustrating all the aspects of life, including the sadness that is both unavoidable and also the stairway to joy.

To restore the painting to its original beauty, we have to fill in that area from which we have unconsciously removed her energy.

Keeping that image un-whole by creating a hole is a lose-lose situation, and so is holding your mother's grief. Of course, we want to help her, but not in this way. Giving her back her energy is the highest, best win-win scenario for you to feel unburdened and for her to feel whole!

How will I know she won't be overwhelmed when we return what's hers?

That's why we do the work. We ask her. We open up a line of dialogue with her and ask her for permission.

Oh, no! I have to talk to her about this?

Yes and no. What we are doing is calling in her Higher Self. The dialogue we create is metaphysical. This type of connection can happen if your mom (or whoever you do this exercise with) is in the next room, an adjacent country, thousands of miles away, or deceased.

This process is usually a lot easier with a partner or teammate there to assist, as discussed in prior chapters. But if that's not possible, just do your best on your own.

Invite your mom's Higher Self to come to you. This can take a few moments, so be patient. Remember the Universe supports your healing. Let her Higher Self emerge without trying to force it. It can show up visually, viscerally, or even verbally. The entire process has the potential of being highly emotional (which isn't necessary; I'm just helping you prepare for all contingencies). Let it be what and how it needs to be.

When her Higher Self arrives, talk to her. Tell her that you love her. Open your heart to the image, feeling, emotion, or even color-shape that has emerged. Then tell her what's true. Tell her that you've been holding her grief, potentially for a very long time. Perhaps you've been holding it so much that it's become the new pattern. So be it. But this doesn't serve you any longer. Tell her that. Also tell her it doesn't serve her, either. If it feels right, you can apologize for holding her back (assuming you do feel sorry—if not, don't lie to your mommy!).

Take the time needed to feel this connection deeply. Superficial connections create superficial healing. Tell her that this is a way you learned to connect when you were younger and that it may have served you in the past but no longer does. Let this awareness deepen within you. Verbalize and feel, "This energy was never mine to carry."

Why can't I just give the energy back to the Universe? Surely, the Universe knows what to do with it!

Well, you could.

Or why can't I just cut the cords?

Well, you could, but in my experience, those are not as effective as Return to Sender. While for some people, giving it back to the Universe or cutting cords may seem more compassionate, I submit that not only are those techniques less compassionate but they're the quicker, seemingly easier, and therefore the less transformative method.

By doing the Return to Sender as described here, you're a more active participant in the healing. You are acting from a new awareness and creating new pathways. You are announcing to yourself, your teammate (if present), and the Universe that being an energetic sponge is a detail in a contract that is now past its expiration date. Feel into that! Doesn't that feel more empowering?!? We're here to not only learn but to live our new learning, and then to share it. *Capisce*?

When it feels right, ask her for permission to return the energy to her.

If She Says Yes

Think about turning on a water faucet. There is no need to push, pull, or force it out. The pressure is already there and naturally moves from an area of higher pressure to an area of lower pressure. Similarly, the energy stuck within you has created pressure. When you ask her Higher Self for permission to return the energy to her and she says yes, open your body or the area where the energy is being held, even a little bit, and open a valve in your mind's eye.

Allow the energy to travel from you to her with love and compassion, never with blame or resentment. Why would you blame her for what you unconsciously decided to keep for her? That makes no sense. The transfer of energy could take three minutes or 30 minutes. Let it do what it has to. Your mind will drift, and that's okay. Just notice that, and bring your focus back to the transfer. Sometimes placing a hand on the affected area can serve as a reminder of what you're doing and create a more tangible point to focus on.

Your mind will also tell you that you're done before you are. That's normal. Stay with the return until you feel something shift! You'll know you are done when the transfer stops. You'll feel something shift within you, indicating the process for this level is complete. At this point, most people report an openness, inner peace, a better sense of balance, calm, even bliss. Physical symptoms that may have been flaring are reduced or eliminated.

Sometimes, the process has to be repeated several times before the entire shift is complete. Be careful not to do too much in one sitting. As a Highly Sensitive Person, you already know your potential for energetic overload. Things that barely affect others can knock us off our feet. Be patient, and trust your guidance to tell you when to continue or when to let everything settle in. Or perhaps your teammate or a practitioner can feel this clearer than you can.

If She Says No

Let's stay with the above scenario to discuss the other possibility. You've done the body scan and are now hyper aware that you're holding your mom's grief in your heart chakra. You call in her Higher Self and explain to her what's going on. You tell her that this is a way you learned to connect with her when you were younger and that it may have served you back then but no longer does. You tell her that your good intentions have resulted in pain and illness for you. You request permission to give her back her energy, remembering that it is hers to deal with. Everything is going great until she says . . . no!

Now what?

This is typically your own resistance manifested outward, and is the end result of one or both of these two questions:

1. Will she really be okay if I return this to her?
2. Who will I be without this energy?

Let's look at, "Will she be okay if I return this to her?"

What is quite burdensome for you is often the proverbial drop in the bucket for her. Because it's hers, not yours, it will seem heavier within you. This heaviness can minimize your desire to carry out Return to Sender and increase your fears about what may happen to her. In this case, if you have a strong connection with her Higher Self, ask her directly! "Will you be okay if I return this to you?"

If the connection is good, her Higher Self will always say yes. If it still does not, it could be more of your own resistance manifesting externally.

So if her Higher Self will always say yes, why do I have to go through all these steps?

I hear you. I've looked for the shortcut for decades, until I realized it wasn't getting me what I wanted. It won't. The shortcut does not always work and typically bypasses the learning opportunity.

The Body Scan and Return to Sender tools are analytical as much as healing tools. Without using the steps as indicated, you will never know if you have resistance to the work—which is as much about growth as it is about healing! Just do the work. If you do it well, Mom's "no" will turn into a "yes." Then, allow the energy to go back to her.

Now, let's look at and answer the next most popular form of resistance, "Who will I be without this energy?"

Sit with the inquiry. Eventually, you may hear or feel the answer. But even if that's difficult, imagine for a moment how it would feel if you were no longer carrying around—in this example, at least—your mother's grief.

You may not have an answer for this question. You could have been carrying others' energy since birth. Hard to imagine what's never been part of your experience, right?

Instead, try answering the following:

"Without this pattern, I will be _____ (fill in the blank)."

Most people say they'll be more themselves (whoever that may be). I often hear descriptive words like "free, open, connected, and in the flow," and those are all true! They have to be. Without all those absorbed layers, you'll have more access to your heart, to your truth, and to deeper, more amazing connections!

Breathe into this potential reality. Sit in the excitement of healing to manifest a better outcome. Show your body how freedom might feel by visualizing it. When that feels as if it's sunk in, ask her once again, and her "no" will likely have turned into a "yes."

Knowing these possibilities, try the Return to Sender exercise once again. Where you were stuck, you'll now be flowing. Where you were frustrated, you'll now be accepting. Where you were unhealthy, you will now be vibrant!

Of course, there may be other forms of resistance, but these are the most common.

If the Body Scan reveals a combination of your energy and that of others, try to feel which one your body wants to work on first. For example if you intuit you're holding your dad's anger and your own grief, feel deeper in to see which one needs work first. If you hear/see/feel to work on dad's anger first, do so using the above steps. Then, work on your own grief using the steps in the next chapter.

6

Healing What's Yours Using Integration

If the Body Scan shows a pain, illness, or energetic blockage that is your own, obviously there is no one to give it back to. Your first reaction may be to get rid of what's there. That's the pattern, not the truth.

Huh?

We live in a world filled with instant gratification. And ever since we were small, few if any of us have had enough safe space to have and express our feelings. Babies are given a pacifier to stop them from crying. Anger in children is often met with anger from an adult—anything to stop the child from expressing emotion. Keeping us small teaches us to repress our emotions. Sadness? Bad. Anger? Very bad. And as we age, our emotional shutdown keeps us from truly connecting with other people, Spirit, and ourselves. We learn to censure these emotions, which ironically, keeps them in place, festering, and ultimately creating energetic blockages leading to pain and illness.

When we finally realize that what we've been doing hasn't worked as well as we'd like it to, we search for deeper ways to heal. Eventually, we realize our own repression is the cause of much of our pain and illness. And ultimately, we learn that we have to face our past. There is no more time for denial, burying, or ignorance. You know too much for any of that.

Sadly, we still have the mindset that we learned while growing up, that pain is bad and we should do anything to alleviate it. This is echoed in TV and print ads for medications, as well. We want a quick fix. We want to fight what's arisen. But as mentioned earlier, fighting increases tension, and to get something accomplished often means to do the exact opposite of what we've been taught. The opposite of tension is acceptance and unconditional love.

Wait? You want me to unconditionally love my pain?

No. I want you—implore you—to love yourself. And your pain is a message to do so. Illness and pain are often end results of not meeting your life challenges head on. It is time to confront your obstacles, ideally, from a place of gratitude.

Riiiight. Now you want me to be grateful for my pain?

No. I want you to be grateful for the opportunity that your pain has shown you. If you've been burying anger for so long it has tightened your muscles, I invite you to look at and heal the anger. The muscles will relax in time, when they get the message your anger is healed—when they feel safe enough to relax.

Similarly, if you've been repressing grief for so long that is has resulted in "me-pression" I invite you to welcome your sadness.

Sadness is inevitable. Some people deny it; others repress it. Because others judged our grief in the past, we learned to judge and repress it, too. Because we learned it wasn't safe to cry or emote, we buried our sadness within. Each time we felt sad, we judged it once again, burying it even farther. We had to work extra hard to keep it under control.

As we grew older, additional systems of thought may have been added on top of the ones we were born into. Some of those systems taught that if we just understood any given situation, we wouldn't have anything to grieve. *Voilà!* Grief, be gone! Grandma's dead? Nothing left to see here. Move along. Other systems taught that we could bypass raw human emotions. They claimed we could pray for forgiveness, or via even more reason and logic, we could let it roll off our backs, letting the energy vanish into thin air.

But for empaths, our backs aren't slippery. And we can feel what's in the air. Neither of these systems has been very effective in the long run. If you look at the pervasiveness of me-pression, you can see that how we've attempted to deal with sadness isn't working. Emotions can't be healed or escaped using logic, reason, or denial of our humanity, nor can they be covered up using chemicals. Even Vulcans like Mr. Spock, who claim to have mastered emotions via logic, become irrational every seven years during Pon Farr, the mating ritual. Ahem.

So if denial, burying, mentalizing, spiritualizing, and judgment don't work, what does? You guessed it: love. I've been shown that we have to meet our emotions. We have to accept them as part of us, rather than believe we are defined by them. Similar to the jigsaw puzzle mentioned earlier, we are made up of all parts, all colors, and yes, all of the emotions. The whole makes us who we are, and I like to believe that who we are is pretty amazing.

Try on this mantra:

> I have sadness, but it does not define me.
>
> I have anger, but it does not define me.
>
> I have jealousy, but it does not define me.
>
> I have joy, but it does not define me.
>
> I have bliss, but it does not define me.
>
> I have love, but love does not define me.
>
> I cannot be defined by my experience.
>
> I am everything, and everything is me.

When our emotional body is activated by life's events, we should accept that we've been triggered and lean into the emotions. Meaning, do not judge what is happening or how we are reacting to it. We should let ourselves have our feelings. Granted, in certain situations we may not feel safe enough to express our feelings, but when possible we should let it rip!

And we should "train" those around us that we don't need to be fixed or reasoned with when our emotional body has been activated. Particularly when we have been triggered, we need empathy, not empowerment; compassion, not discussion. Tell those close to you what you need. As long as you're not making them wrong for not knowing what you need, most people will appreciate the information and comply with your request! Teach others how to hold safe space for you! Modeling safe space for their feelings may be returned in kind.

Think of sadness or anger as a lack of unconditional love. How do we heal the absence of unconditional love? With . . .

unconditional love! We let the emotions be there. We sit with them. Invite them for tea. We witness them unconditionally. Anything but condemn them, please.

I think of this like an ice cube in the sun. If the sun could speak, it wouldn't say, "You're frozen, cold and hard. I don't like that about you, I'm going to melt you into being softer." No. The sun shines its light, and the ice cube naturally melts into liquid. Both the liquid and the solid are water, just in different forms. So it is with energy. Sadness is a form of energy and can be "melted" with another form of energy, love.

Most of us have no idea how much sadness and anger we've buried. When I see my clients release years of sadness I'm amazed at how they could even walk considering how much had been held.

The most common fear with accessing our repressed sadness is that if we let ourselves feel the deepest levels of despair, we'll never return. We'll be stuck in the dumps. Ironically, the exact opposite is true. And as true as this is, don't expect someone you know and love to sit with what they've been judging as bad, possibly for decades. As much as you know this to be effective, we have to meet people where they are. Someone who grew up believing that sadness should never be shown would scoff at the idea of releasing it being healthy.

But the proof is in the pudding, as they say. Those who befriend their sadness can lift themselves out of me-pression. Those who honor and accept their anger and befriend it can release their tight muscles and alleviate many other symptoms associated with repressed anger. Those who honor their shadow selves are more capable of expressing their light.

Begin the process by setting an intention out loud. Say it like you mean it. Better yet, mean it:

My intention is to invite into my conscious awareness that which has been buried.

I do not criticize myself for burying the emotion of the past. That is what I had to do at that time. Nor do I judge the content of the emotion. But now, in this safe space, I ask to be shown what is within me.

As you and your teammate sit in silence with openness and curiosity, the layer that is ready to be healed will rise and come into your consciousness. It may look a certain way—for example you may see an image, a color, even a long-forgotten memory. Your attention may also be brought to a specific area in your body.

It is likely that this process won't feel very good, and you may wish you had never started it. That's normal. But challenge yourself to stay with what emerges, knowing that it has been stuck within you and out of conscious awareness. The more one stays with what's happening from a place of curiosity and openness, the easier the entire process becomes. Remember, resistance only adds to the existing tension. Remind yourself that you survived it going in and you will survive it coming out!

No, it's not always fun. No, it's not always easy. But it is simple. And if we can accept the roller-coaster of healing, which naturally includes all the ups and downs, we can also accept our reactions to those hills and valleys. The question is, Are we going to white-knuckle the ride or trust we're taken care of? Can we wave our hands in the air and welcome the ups and downs?

My guess is that you've read many books or done many practices to manage your emotions. But if you're reading this, perhaps those haven't worked as well as you'd hoped. That's not to disrespect you, the authors, healers, or their practices; it's just my observation based on having studied, experienced, and sometimes taught so many different modalities.

They all brought us to this moment, and in this moment, all of us can celebrate the journey and the challenges that brought us here. No matter how hard those challenges were, you're still here, so you've done something right. Perhaps what I've described in this book is the next step for you; perhaps, not. I invite you to embrace whatever is true for you.

Return to Sender and Integration may need to be done daily or weekly. Try to let your body tell you what it can handle and when by using the Body Scan. If you attempt the Body Scan and nothing arises, try again at another time. You're not wrong or bad if the exercise doesn't produce the desired effect. Our bodies know more than our minds do, so let's give them credit.

As you continually state your intention to heal what's there in your daily affirmations, meditations, and conversations, your body will get the message. As you write about, feel into, or talk about your understanding of what needs to happen for you to heal, eventually the Body Scan, Return to Sender, and Integration will flow with more ease.

Trust the timing of the entire process. Recognize that some information has been kept within you until you have the tools and the safe space to work with them. Then create safe space, and cultivate curiosity and willingness to do whatever it takes to heal.

7

Recalibration

The potential for transferring and healing vast amounts of energy using the Return to Sender or Integration exercises can shake up your inner world. But, like a recently shaken snow globe, in time the loose flakes will settle down to form a new landscape. Actively reducing the distance between shaking and settling is called Recalibration.

After an intense session that includes Return to Sender and/or Integration, we should give the body time to adjust to the new status quo. To recalibrate on your own, give yourself some downtime. Meditation or just lying down are great, but journaling is preferable. Write down what just happened as best as you can remember. Note how you felt before, during, and after. Or just let your pen do its thing. In addition to Recalibration, be open to obtaining new insights and clarity that can quite often only come because you've been opened from doing the healing work.

Recalibration can also be done with a teammate or healer. Have the teammate continue to hold the safe space that they did during the work, and set a clear intention to metabolize all that's been transferred or healed.

Your left brain may hate this, but you don't have to *do* anything!

Trust the body's innate healing capacity and ability to embody what's been done a few moments earlier. Let the two (or more) of you sit together in silence, allowing what needs to happen. Stay with the process until it feels complete, noticing when the mind is sick of the silence or has moved onto, "What's next?' Then, with love and compassion, ask your body if you really are complete. If not, continue the process.

When the process of Recalibration is finished, thank your teammate in whatever way has been agreed upon or in a way that feels appropriate.

I know the above sounds simple; it is. And I know the above may not sound very specific. But the cookbook-style diagnosis, prognosis, and treatments are part of what got us into more pain due to their unrealistic expectations and inability to allow for individuality.

Recalibration needn't be arduous. By the time you get to this step, the more challenging work has already been done. Think of this like a zero-calorie, zero-guilt dessert! Just enjoy this Recalibration and the new you, inclusive of more joy, more openness, increased vitality, and symptom-free living!

Conclusion

An amazing thing happens when we fully understand that we've been a sponge for the energies and emotions of others: We have a visceral, tangible experience of our interconnectedness.

This oneness we often hear about sounds great, but our physical senses will tell us otherwise! By continuing our inner work, as described in this book or other books and practices, we can learn to embody this sense of oneness, which is beyond conscious understanding. This higher truth can become a template for an expressed unity between individuals—and ultimately, groups of many types—bringing peace to a war-torn history and present-day experience, leading to a more united future.

Do you know what I find even more amazing? That everyone is born connected to the All, of which we are an intrinsic part. Everyone is empathic. It's only our experiences that help us remember or block or forget our empathic nature and interconnectedness.

Once we open to consciously remembering this, our whole world changes. We desire more than ever to share our love and compassion with others, partly because we understand that by loving others we are also loving ourselves. This awareness, along with practicing the tools in *Empathipedia*, can open our hearts in a safe manner, spreading the message of oneness with our thoughts, words, and actions. Others will feel your lightness and your new-found radiance.

Together, we can trust that as each one of us does our small part in opening to being and expressing more love, others will be inspired to do the same. As we exhibit a calm, centered, and vibrant self, others will eventually ask us how we attained that state. My intention is that this book has been a catalyst to heal what ails you and has deepened your experience and expression of oneness!

And so it is.

Dave's Services and Contact Info

Dave Markowitz works in one-on-one and group settings. Each can be done in person or remotely via phone or video.

His first book on this subject and second overall, the best-selling self-published *Self-Care for the Self-Aware: A Guide for Highly Sensitive People, Empaths, Intuitives, and Healers* was on Amazon's Top 20 for 41 consecutive months in its category.

His first book, the best-selling *Healing with Source: A Spiritual Guide to Mind-Body Medicine* originally published by Findhorn Press and now carried by Inner Traditions, hit number 3 in its category on Amazon in its first week of availability.

Dave's work has been endorsed by best-selling authors Shirley MacLaine, Lynn Andrews, Dannion and Kathryn Brinkley, and Dr. Meg Blackburn Losey, and he's lectured with luminaries such as Deepak Chopra and Gary Null.

For more information and to contact Dave, or to sign up for his newsletter to be the first to know about discounts, tele-workshops, events in your area and so on, see www.DaveMarkowitz.com.

Printed in the United States
By Bookmasters